CDs, Super Glue, and Salsa

HOW EVERYDAY PRODUCTS ARE MADE

CDs,
Super Glue,
and Salsa

HOW EVERYDAY
PRODUCTS ARE
MADE

Volume 1
A – K

An imprint of Gale Research Inc.,
an International Thomson Publishing Company

I(T)P

NEW YORK • LONDON • BONN • BOSTON • DETROIT • MADRID
MELBOURNE • MEXICO CITY • PARIS • SINGAPORE • TOKYO
TORONTO • WASHINGTON • ALBANY NY • BELMONT CA • CINCINNATI OH

CD's, Super Glue, and Salsa: How Everyday Products Are Made
Sharon Rose and Neil Schlager

Staff
Kathleen L. Witman, U•X•L Assistant Developmental Editor
Carol DeKane Nagel, U•X•L Developmental Editor
Thomas L. Romig, U•X•L Publisher

Margaret A. Chamberlain, Permissions Specialist (Pictures)

Catherine Kemp, Production Assistant
Evi Seoud, Assistant Production Manager
Mary Beth Trimper, Production Director

Mark Howell, Page and Cover Designer
Cynthia Baldwin, Art Director

The Graphix Group, Typesetting

Library of Congress Cataloging-in-Publication Data
CD's, super glue, and salsa : how everyday products are made / edited by Sharon Rose.
     p. cm.
Includes bibliographical references and indexes.
Contents: v. 1. A-K — v. 2. L-Z
ISBN 0-8103-9791-9 (set). — ISBN 0-8103-9792-7 (v. 1). —ISBN 0-8103-9793-5 (v. 2).
1. Manufactures—Juvenile literature. [1. Manufactures.]
I. Rose, Sharon.
TS146.C37 1995
670—dc20

94-35243
CIP
AC

This book is printed on acid-free paper that meets the minimum requirements of American National Standard for information Sciences—Permanence Paper for Printed Library Materials, ANSI Z39.48-1984.

Printed in the United States of America

I(T)P™ U·X·L is an imprint of Gale Research Inc.,
    an International Thomson Publishing Company.
    ITP logo is a trademark under license.   10 9 8 7 6 5 4 3 2

Contents

Reader's Guide

CD's, Super Glue, and Salsa: How Everyday Products Are Made is written for a generation born into a fast-moving world of sophisticated electronics and space-age technology. So many common products used at home or in school are complex, automated, push-button, instant access, computerized, microwaved wonders. Simple, streamlined outward appearances disguise the difficult steps taken to imagine, invent, create, and manufacture them.

CD's, Super Glue, and Salsa reveals the mysteries behind popular foods and comfortable clothes, complex machinery and creative conveniences. The items selected represent progress and fashion trends that influence industry, transportation, music, diet, entertainment, and lifestyle. Detailed, step-by-step descriptions of processes, simple explanations of technical terms and concepts, and helpful illustrations and photographs highlight each entry.

Format

The 30 entries in *CD's, Super Glue, and Salsa* are arranged alphabetically in two volumes. Although the focus of each entry is the manufacturing process, a wealth of related information is provided: who invented the product or how it has developed, how it works, from what materials it is made, how it is designed, quality control procedures, future applications, and a list of books and periodicals on where to find more information.

To make it easier to locate areas of interest, the entries are broken up into several sections. Most entries include sections devoted to information about the following:

- Background—history or development

- Raw materials needed for production

- Design of the product—how it works

- Manufacturing process

- Quality control
- Byproducts
- Future products
- Where to learn more

Additonal Features

Boxed sections and call-outs provide related or special interest facts about a product or its development. More than 60 illustrations and 100 photos supplement the written information. Each volume also contains a general subject index with important terms, processes, materials, and people.

Comments and Suggestions

We welcome comments on this work as well as suggestions for other products to be featured in future editions of *CD's, Super Glue, and Salsa* Please write: Editor, *CD's, Super Glue, and Salsa*, U•X•L, 835 Penobscot Bldg., Detroit, Michigan 48226-4094; call toll-free: 1-800-877-4253; or fax: 313-961-6348.

Photo Credits

Photographs and illustrations appearing in *CDs, Super Glue, and Salsa: How Everyday Products Are Made,* were received from the following sources:

©Alan Oddie/Photo Edit: pp. 1, 27; UPI/Bettmann: pp. 3, 82, 192; The Bettmann Archive: pp. 4, 37, 90, 92; ©Dick Luria 1989/FPG International: p. 5; ©David Young-Wolff/Photo Edit: pp. 12, 91, 165, 191, 194, 195, 247, 248; ©1985 Jan Staller/The Stock Market: p. 13; ©1992 Bill Losh/FPG International: p. 17; ©Tony Freeman/Photo Edit: pp. 20, 21, 67, 74, 152, 161, 169, 179, 181, 184, 200, 201, 219, 220, 229, 230, 238, 239, 265, 273, 279; FPG International: pp. 22, 56; Courtesy Levi Straus and Company: p. 28; ©Art Tilley/FPG International: p. 29; ©Gary Connor/Photo Edit: pp. 36, 263; ©Ulf Sjostedt 1990/FPG International: p. 39; Reuters/Bettmann: pp. 46, 48, 117, 212, 271; Illustration by Daniel D. Feaser: p. 47; Brownie Harris/The Stock Market: p. 50; ©Roy Morsch 1988/The Stock Market: p. 54; ©1989 Connie Hansen/The Stock Market: p. 57; ©1982 Charles Schneider/FPG International: p. 62; ©David Hundley/The Stock Market: p. 63; ©Barry Rosenthal Studio, Inc./FPG International: p. 64; ©1989 Thomas Lindsay/FPG International: p. 65; ©Jeffrey Sylvester/FPG International: pp. 73, 137; ©Tom McCarthy Photos, Model Released 1993/Photo Edit: p. 79; ©Thierry Cariou/The Stock Market: p. 80; ©Pete Saloutos 1994/The Stock Market: p. 81; ©Michael Krasowitz 1993/FPG International: p. 89; ©1985 Paul Ambrose/FPG International: pp. 98, 100; ©1985 Dick Luria/FPG International: p. 99; ©Richard Laird 1989/FPG International: pp. 107, 255, 256; ©Chris Sorensen/The Stock Market: pp. 109, 113; ©1993 Richard Mackson/FPG International: p. 112; ©Phil McCarten/Photo Edit: p. 115; ©1991 Jim McNee/FPG International: p. 116; AP/Wide World Photos: pp. 119, 146, 257; ©1991 Ken Korsh/FPG International: p. 138; ©Myrleen Ferguson Cate/Photo Edit: p. 139; ©1989 Ron Scott/The Stock Market: pp. 145, 148; ©1989 John Gillmore/The Stock Market: pp. 154, 155; Courtesy of Bob Huffman: p. 157; ©Peter Johansky/FPG International: p. 164; Don Mason/The Stock Market: p. 172; ©1985 Michael A. Keller/FPG International: p. 174; ©Roy Morsch/The Stock Market: p. 205; From *Earth-*

Automobile

History

Etienne Lenoir, a mechanic from Belgium, was the first to introduce the combustion engine (an engine that changes heat into motion by the expansion of fuel burned inside) in 1860. During the next few decades, inventors concentrated on making vehicles using this or other types of engines. As demand for automobiles quickly exceeded supply, inventors, especially Henry Ford, turned their talents toward speeding up and streamlining automobile production with the first assembly line.

Henry Ford demonstrated his first experimental vehicle, the Quadricycle (a four-wheeled motorized bicycle), in 1896.

Ford's Better Idea

Ford's first attempt at automobile assembly began with the Model A in 1903. The entire vehicle was put together (often by just one person) on a nonmoving assembly stand. Ford had parts delivered as needed. After building a number of different models, Ford developed the Model T. This model was an ingenious design that required fewer parts as well as fewer skilled workers, a tremendous advantage over his competition. During this car's assembly, Ford had decided to use multiple assembly platforms with workers moving from stand to stand, each performing a specific task. This process reduced assembly time for each task from 8.5 hours to a mere 2.5 minutes because each worker only had to learn one specific job.

Ford soon realized that walking from stand to stand wasted time and created traffic jams when faster workers piled up behind slower ones. In Detroit, Michigan, in 1913, he solved this problem by introducing the first moving assembly line, a conveyor that moved a vehicle past a stationary worker. By eliminating the need for workers to move between stations, Ford cut the task time for each worker from 2.5 minutes to less than 2 minutes. More Model Ts rolled off Ford's assembly line in one week than his competitors, using the older methods, could produce in a whole year.

The first conveyor line consisted of metal strips to which the vehicle's wheels were attached. The strips were attached to a belt that rolled the length of the factory and then, beneath the floor, returned to the starting point. By the 1920s, Ford could produce one Model T every 10 seconds—more than 800 per day.

This dramatic reduction of time and effort required to assemble an automobile drew the interest of manufacturers throughout the world. Ford's mass production methods dominated the automobile industry for decades and were eventually adopted by almost every other manufacturing industry. Although modern technology has made many improvements possible in today's auto plants, the basic concept of the first assembly line has not changed. Stationary auto workers still install parts on vehicles that roll past work stations arranged in a long, winding line.

Steel vs. Plastic

Most automobile parts are made of strong steel, but petroleum-based products (plastics and vinyls) are becoming popular, light-weight alternatives. Plastic parts have lightened some models by as much as 30 percent. As the price of fuel continues to rise, car drivers are buying lighter, more fuel efficient vehicles.

Setting Styles

Introducing a new model of automobile generally takes three to five years of planning and testing. Ideas for new models come from designers' efforts to anticipate the needs and preferences of the public. Trying to pre-

Henry Ford in 1924 with the first and 10 millionth manufactured Ford Model T.

dict what drivers will need and want to drive in five years is no small task, yet auto companies continue to successfully design cars that catch consumers' fancy.

With the help of computerized design equipment, design engineers develop basic concept drawings to illustrate the proposed vehicle's appearance. Then they construct clay models to be studied by styling experts. Other engineers review the models, studying air-flow patterns and determining how the design will hold up under required crash tests. Once the models have been reviewed and accepted, tool designers begin to build the tools that will manufacture the parts of the new model.

The Manufacturing Process

Components

1 The automobile assembly plant is the final phase in the process of manufacturing an automobile. It is here that the components (mechanical parts) supplied by more than 4,000 outside suppliers are

Ford Motor Company assembly line workers dropping an engine into a Model T chassis in 1913.

brought together, usually by truck or train, for assembly. Those parts that will be used in the chassis (frame) are delivered to one area, while parts which will make up the auto body are unloaded at another.

Chassis

2 The typical car or truck is constructed from the ground up. The chassis (see fig. 1) forms the rectangular, strong base on which the body rests. The frame is placed on the assembly line and clamped to the conveyor to prevent shifting as it moves down the line. From here the automobile frame moves to component assembly areas where complete front and rear sections, gas tanks, rear axles (parts which hold and support wheels), drive shafts, gear boxes, steering box parts, wheel drums, and braking systems are installed one after another.

A 1989 Porsche 911.

3 At this stage, an off-line operation matches the vehicle's engine with its transmission (an assembly of gears and other parts which relays power from the engine to the driving axle). Workers use robotic arms to install these heavy parts inside the engine area of the frame. After the engine and transmission are installed, a worker attaches the radiator (an engine cooling device), and another bolts it into place.

Because these parts are heavy and delicate, robots lift, carry, and join them while human workers use power tools to bolt the pieces in place. Careful studies of every assembly task ensure that workers use the safest and most efficient tools available.

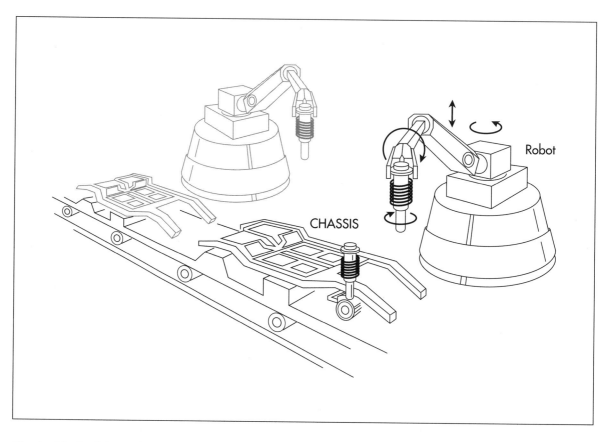

Fig. 1. Much of the work on auto assembly lines is now done by robots rather than humans. In the first stages of auto manufacture, robots weld (join) the floor pan pieces together and assist workers in placing other parts onto the chassis.

Body

4 Generally, the floor pan is the largest body part to which a multitude of panels and braces will be welded or bolted. As it moves down the assembly line, clamped in place, the shell of the vehicle is built. First, the left and right quarter panels are robotically attached to the floor pan, then welded in place (see fig. 1).

5 The front and rear door pillars, roof, and body side panels are assembled in the same fashion (see fig. 2). Robots are especially useful to human workers in this operation because of the ease and accuracy with which they can join these large, heavy pieces. Robots can pick up and load a 200-pound roof panel in precisely the proper weld

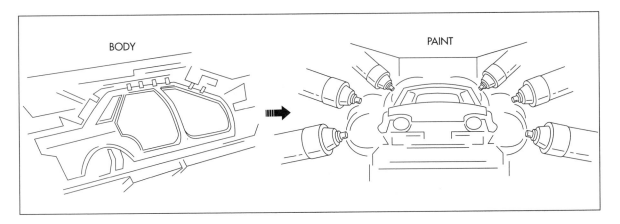

Fig. 2. The body is built up on a separate assembly line from the chassis. Once the body shell is complete, it is attached to an overhead conveyor for a multi-step painting process. This involves inspection, cleaning, undercoat dipping, drying, top-coat spraying, and baking.

position. Robots can also better tolerate the heat, smoke, bright flashes, and gases created during this welding phase.

6 As the body moves from the weld area of the assembly line, other body components are added. They include fully assembled doors, deck lids, hood panel, fenders, trunk lid, and bumper reinforcements. Although robots help workers place these parts onto the body shell, workers provide the proper fit for most of the bolt-on parts using power tools.

Paint

7 Before painting, the body must pass a rigorous inspection process— the body in white operation. The shell of the vehicle passes through a brightly lit white room where it is fully wiped down by inspectors using cloths soaked in hi-light oil. Under the lights, this oil allows inspectors to see any defects in the sheet metal body panels. Dings, dents, and any other defects are repaired right on the line by skilled body repairmen. After the shell has been fully inspected and repaired, the assembly conveyor carries it through a cleaning station where it is immersed and cleaned of all oil, dirt, and contaminants.

Originally, cars were available only in black. Black was the color of choice because of its chemical makeup—it dried much faster than other colors. In 1924 a new, fast-drying paint called duco lacquer was invented and a rainbow of car colors followed.

8 As the body shell exits the cleaning station it passes through a drying booth and then through an undercoat dip (a bath of undercoat paint called the E-coat), which covers every nook and cranny of the body shell, both inside and out, with primer (an undercoat paint which prepares a surface for final painting).

9 After the E-coat bath, the shell is again dried in a booth as it proceeds to the final paint operation. In most automobile assembly plants today, vehicle bodies are spray-painted by robots programmed to apply the exact amounts of paint to just the right areas for just the right length of time (see fig. 2). Considerable research and programming has gone into the dynamics of robotic painting in order to ensure the shiny "wet look" finishes consumers have come to expect. Robotic painters are a big improvement on the process used for Ford's first Model Ts, which were painted by hand with a brush.

10 Once the shell has been fully covered with a base coat of color paint and a clear top coat, the conveyor transfers the bodies through baking ovens where the paint is cured (finished, set) at temperatures over 275 degrees Fahrenheit (135 degrees Celsius). After the shell leaves the paint area it is ready for interior assembly.

Interior assembly

11 The painted shell proceeds through the interior assembly area, where workers add such details as instrumentation and wiring systems, dash panels, interior lights, seats, door and trim panels, headliners, radio, speakers, all glass except the windshield, steering column and wheel, body weatherstrips, vinyl tops, brake and gas pedals, and carpeting.

12 Next, robots equipped with suction cups remove the windshield from a shipping container, apply a line of a glue-like sealer to the edge of the glass, and place it into the windshield frame. Robots also pick up seats and trim panels and transport them to the vehicle for the ease and efficiency of the worker. After passing through this section, the shell is given a water test to ensure the proper fit of door panels, glass, and weatherstripping. It is now ready to mate (join) the chassis.

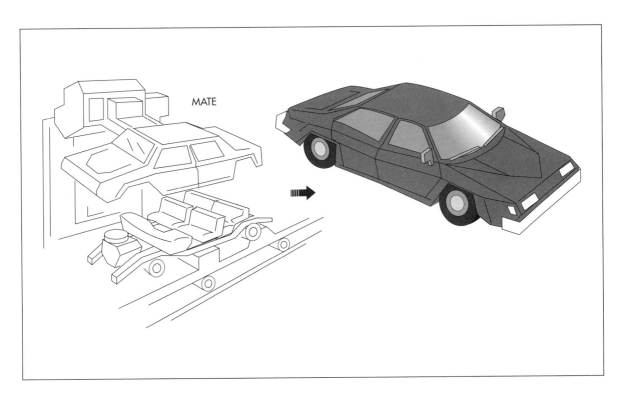

MATE

Fig. 3.   The body and chassis assemblies are mated near the end of the production process. Robotic arms lift the body shell onto the chassis frame, where human workers then bolt the two together. After final components are installed, the vehicle is driven off the assembly line to a quality checkpoint.

Mate

13 The chassis assembly conveyor and the body shell conveyor meet at this stage of production (see fig. 3). As the chassis passes the body conveyor the shell is robotically lifted and placed onto the car frame. Assembly workers, some at ground level and some in work pits beneath the conveyor, bolt the car body to the frame. Once the mating takes place the automobile moves down the line to receive final trim, battery, tires, anti-freeze, and gasoline.

14 The vehicle can now be started. From here a worker drives it to a checkpoint off the line, where other workers examine and adjust the engine, check its lights and horn, balance the tires, and test its charging system. Any defects discovered at this stage require that the car be taken to a central repair area, usually located near the end of the line. A crew of skilled trouble-shooters analyze and repair all problems. When the vehicle passes this final exam it is given a price label and driven to a staging lot where it will await shipment to its destination.

Quality Control

All of the components that go into the automobile are produced at other locations. This means the thousands of mechanical parts that go into a car must be manufactured, tested, packaged, and shipped to the assembly plants, often on the same day they will be used. This requires an enormous amount of planning. To accomplish it, most automobile manufacturers require vendors (outside companies that sell these parts) to subject their components to the same rigorous testing and inspection used in auto plants. This way assembly plants can expect that the products arriving from other manufacturers are approved and free from defects.

Each new automobile is assigned a Vehicle Identification Number (VIN) at the start of the assembly line. This allows production control specialists to trace the progress of each model as well as the source of its components. Throughout the assembly process there are quality check points where vital information is recorded concerning the function of various components.

This idea came from the changes in quality control over the years. Formerly, quality control was seen as a final inspection, checking for defects only after the vehicle was built. In contrast, today quality is seen as a process built into the design of the vehicle as well as the assembly process. This allows assembly operators to stop the conveyor if a defect is found. Corrections can then be made, or supplies checked to determine whether an entire batch of components is defective. Vehicle recalls are costly and manufacturers do everything possible to guarantee their product before it is sold.

At the end of the assembly line all of the quality checks are validated. Final tests are made to catch any defects, squeaks and rattles, improperly fitting panels, or malfunctioning electrical parts. In many assembly plants vehicles are periodically pulled from the line and given full functional tests. Every effort is made to ensure the quality and reliability of the automobiles.

Future Attractions

The growth of automobile use and the increasing difficulty and expense of road building have made highway systems overcrowded and outdated. New electronic vehicle technologies that permit cars to navigate around traffic jams and even drive themselves may soon be possible. Computerizing automobiles would allow the cars to receive traffic information and map the fastest route to a destination, thus making better use of limited highway space.

Another attraction is the development of the electric automobile—a car that appears closer to reality than ever before. It owes more to innovative solar and aeronautical engineering and advanced satellite and radar technology than to traditional automotive design and construction. The electric car has no engine, exhaust system, transmission, muffler, radiator, or spark plugs. It will require neither tune-ups nor gasoline. Instead, its power will come from high-performance batteries that will be environmentally safe and recyclable. Forecasters predict that in the near future the electric car will soon have its own parking place among gas-powered vehicles.

WHERE TO LEARN MORE

Evans, Arthur. *Automobile*. Lerner Publications Company, 1985.

How Things Are Made. National Geographic Society, 1981.

Reader's Digest: How in the World? Reader's Digest, 1990.

Skurzynski, Gloria. *Robots*. Bradbury Press, 1990.

Willis, Terri, and Wallace Black. *CARS: An Environmental Challenge*. Childrens Press, Chicago, 1992.

Young, Frank. *Automobile: From Prototype to Scrapyard*. Gloucester Press, 1982.

Bar Code Scanner

Supermarket scanners (point-of-sale scanners) are specifically designed to read bar codes on oddly shaped, wet, dirty, or fragile grocery items.

Decoding the Bars

Bar codes—those funny little rows of black and white stripes—are showing up almost everywhere. On magazines, cereal boxes, candy bar wrappers, cars, library cards, even on the back of this book. Where do they come from? What do they mean? And how can a person crack the secret code to read their messages?

Bar codes are interpreted by scanners. The bar code scanner shines light sequentially (one stripe after another down the row) across a bar code, very rapidly. It picks up and records a pattern of reflected and non-reflected light (white stripes reflect light very well, while black stripes reflect hardly any light at all) then translates this pattern into an electrical signal the computer can understand.

The first scanners required human action to do the scanning and used very simple light sources. Clerks had to place the end of a wand scanner directly against the code, because its narrow light source could only tell the difference between bars and stripes right at the wand tip. By the mid 1970s, rotating, motor-driven mirrors allowed a stronger light source, a laser beam, to be swept over a surface so the user didn't need to move the scanner or the object containing the bar code. This technology greatly improved scanner reliability and speed.

A small, hand-held bar code scanner.

Later, holograms (a photographic image that behaves like a three-dimensional object when struck by light) were chosen to replace mirrors, since they act just like a mirror but are lightweight and easily motorized. Whereas earlier scanners worked by rotating a mirror assembly, holographic scanners operate by spinning a disk with one or more holograms recorded on it.

By 1980 holographic point-of-sale scanners were available to businesses. Holographic scanning was preferred because the hologram disks could be spun more easily than mirrors, and because a single disk could reflect light in many different directions, by placing different hologram areas on the same disk. This helped to solve the problem of bar code positioning; that is, codes no longer needed to directly face the scan window.

Modern bar code scanners read in many different directions, hundreds of times each second. If you look at the surface of a scanner in the checkout lane, you will see lots of crisscrossed lines of light. This pattern was chosen as the most reliable and because of its ability to read codes on many different types of packages.

Holograms are created by shining a laser beam split into two parts onto a glass or plastic plate coated with photographic liquids.

Scanner Materials

A holographic bar code scanner consists of a number of preformed parts. The laser—a small glass tube filled with gas and a small power supply to generate a beam—is usually a helium neon (HeNe) laser. In other words, the gas tube is filled with helium and neon gases, which produce a red light. Red light is easiest to detect, and HeNe's are less expensive than other kinds of lasers.

Lenses and mirrors in the scanner are made of highly polished glass or plastic (see fig. 5). The light detection system is a photodiode—a semiconductor that transfers electrical current when light shines on it, and no current when no light is present. Silicon or germanium (crystal-like substances) are the two types of photodiodes most commonly used.

The housing consists of a sturdy case, usually made of stainless steel, and a window of glass or plastic. The window material must remain transparent yet seal the scanner from air, dirt and dust which could block light or the light detector. Defects in the window can cause light to be transmitted incorrectly, causing inaccurate readings.

The holographic disks are made of a substance called dichromated gelatin (DCG) sealed between two plastic disks (see fig. 4). DCG is a light-sensitive chemical used to record laser images, much like photographic film records light. DCG will lose a recorded image if it is left in the open air, which is why it must be sealed between two layers of plastic.

The spinning motor drive that turns the disk is a small electric cylinder with a central spinning shaft, similar to the kind available in an erector (building) set. The shaft is attached to the center of the hologram disk, so that when the motor is turned on, the disk spins.

Scanner Design

Bar code scanners require not just one designer, but an entire team. First, a laser recording engineer designs the hologram disk. An optical engineer then determines the placement of the laser and hologram disk. It is also this engineer's job to fit the scanner parts into the smallest space, with the smallest weight and expense. Next, an electrical engineer determines the best method of interpreting the electrical signals coming from the photodetector (the part which accepts the bar code message and transmits the code to a computer). Finally, a computer programmer must design the computer software that will translate the code into readable product information.

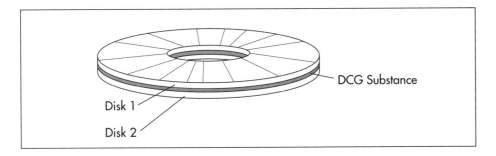

Fig. 4. The spinning holographic disk consists of a chemical substance, DCG, sandwiched between two plastic disks.

The Manufacturing Process

After all these scanner parts and materials have been designed, they are ready to be made and assembled. The hologram disk is generally manufactured by the scanner company, while other parts (lenses, mirrors, and laser) are usually purchased from other manufacturers. The various parts are then assembled and tested.

Hologram disk

1 The first step is to mass produce (make many copies) the hologram disk. This disk is copied from a master hologram. All the disks, master and copies, are sandwiches made of plastic "bread" with DCG filling (see fig. 4). Master disks are made in sections, one wedge for each reflection angle required in the final disk. A typical point-of-sale scanner will have between seven and 16 wedges on a single disk. Each wedge is prepared by recording holographic patterns on the DCG sandwich with two intersecting laser beams. Changing the angle at which the two beams meet will make each wedge act like a mirror that is turned in a different direction.

2 Once all the required wedges are recorded, they are assembled and glued down on a single transparent plate, which can then be copied. This is done by a process called optical replication, which involves placing the master disk very close to a blank DCG sandwich disk, then shining a single laser beam through the master from behind. This transfers the pattern onto the blank disk.

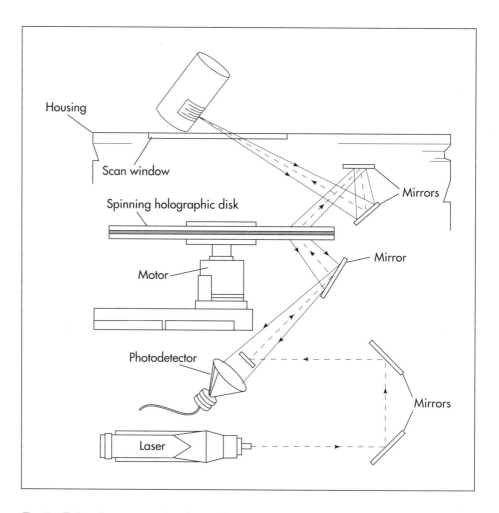

Fig. 5. Follow the arrows... In a bar code scanner, a laser beam is directed toward an item with a black and white bar code symbol, sometimes with the help of angled mirrors. The light is reflected back and recorded on a spinning holographic disk. A photodetector then converts this light into an electrical signal that can be read by a computer.

Lenses, mirrors, laser

3 Other parts—lenses, mirrors, and laser—are manufactured according-ing to designer specifications. The scanner manufacturer tests them as they arrive. Motors and lasers are tested for proper operation and strength, to be sure the bar code scanner will work for a reasonable period of time.

Groceries being scanned at a supermarket.

Housing

4 The housing is simply the container chosen to hold the scanner parts. It can be purchased from a metal job shop, or made by the manufacturer. The size and exact shape of the box are chosen by the designers. Their designs are first converted into realistic sketches, then the parts are machined, assembled, and tested for durability.

Final assembly

5 Finally, the hologram disk is assembled with the spinning motor drive and tested. Scanning pattern, direction, and speed are all examined. The spinning disk is then assembled with the optical system (laser and mirrors). Placement of the laser often depends on space: the beam can be aimed directly at the spinning disk, or at a mirror that guides it to the disk, if this makes the package smaller.

6 The disk and optical system are tested as a unit. When the assembly passes inspection, it is mounted permanently inside the housing and sealed with the scanning window.

Quality Control

Bar code scanners must pass several working tests before earning a stamp of industry approval. Scanners are run for several days (some are subjected to lifetime tests—up to several years) to ensure that the motor will continue to turn the disk consistently at the expected speed. Spinning speed affects ability to differentiate between wide and narrow bars in a code, so it is critical that speed is reliable. This speed may also need to be adjusted to match the rate at which a clerk passes items through a supermarket checkout.

Scanners are also tested for code reading consistency. For a good bar code scanner, this should be greater than 85 percent. If it fails, the scanner is sent back for an inspection of the optical system.

Holographic scanners beam their light over a bar code 100 to 200 times per second. This allows the computer to compare many different readings of the code for accuracy. Part of this test uses bar codes that are imperfect in some way—codes containing ink spots, bars of incorrect width, etc. The manufacturer is expected to produce a scanner that can tolerate some mistakes in the code printing process and still make sense of the code.

Unique Uses of Bar Code Technology

More and more uses of bar code technology crop up all the time. Children with impaired vision are learning braille with the help of bar code technology. Each raised-dot braille entry has a matching bar code beneath it. When a light wand or pen is passed over the code, a computerized voice pronounces the word. This method allows the children to learn braille independently.

Scientists tagged 100 bees with very small bar codes. The code was delicately attached to the thorax (middle section) of a bee with shellac (a clear, glue-like sealer). Combined with a laser scanner at the entrance to their hive, the codes told scientists what time a bee left home, how long it was away, and when the bee returned.

Scanning the Future

Better bar codes are in the works and the scanners that read them must keep pace. Cheaper and smaller light sources will improve simple instruments like the wand scanner. Semiconductor lasers, for instance, may make the wand more popular and practical for users.

Researchers have already developed a two-dimensional (2-D) bar code that stores about 100 times more information in the same amount of space used by the old one-dimensional, straight-line style. The new bar codes are about the size of a postage stamp and look more like a miniature maze than a line of stripes. With this technology, hospitals, for example, could include an entire medical history plus allergy or emergency information on a patient's traditional identification bracelet. The possibilities of information storage are endless.

WHERE TO LEARN MORE

Adams, Russ. *Reading Between the Lines: An Introduction to Bar Code Technology*, 4th ed. Helmers Publishing, 1989.

Alpert, Mark. "Building a Better Bar Code," *Fortune*. June 15, 1992, p. 101.

Macaulay, David. *The Way Things Work*. Houghton Mifflin Company, 1988.

Pennisi, Elizabeth. "Bolder Bar Codes," *Science News*. August 17, 1991, pp. 106-7.

Reader's Digest: How in the World? Reader's Digest, 1990.

Baseball

Approximately 600,000 baseballs are used by all Major League teams combined during one baseball season. The average baseball remains in play for only five to seven pitches in a Major League game.

Batter Up!

Baseball, that all-American symbol of summer fun, had its origins in England in the early 1800s. "Rounders" was the name of the game played by English boys and later imported to New York by businessmen. You had to be tough to play rounders, since outs were made by throwing the ball and actually hitting the runner as he ran between bases. Luckily, a soft ball was used in rounders.

In 1845 Alexander Cartwright of New York wrote the rules for baseball as we know it. Soft balls couldn't be hit very far, nor did they make that nice, satisfying "crack" as they hit a bat. In the name of excitement and safety, Cartwright proposed using a smaller, harder ball, but substituted tagging a runner rather than hitting him for an out.

Despite its simple appearance, the baseball is in fact a precision-made object and has often been the subject of serious controversy. Although baseballs have changed very little in this century, some fans believe the balls have secretly been "juiced up" to increase the number of crowd-pleasing home runs hit during slow seasons. Manufacturers of baseballs and the Major League Baseball organization have steadfastly denied these charges, and no proof of change in the ball's design or materials has ever been revealed.

An official Major League baseball must weigh between 5 and 5.25 ounces (about 141.75-148.83 grams) and measure between 9 and 9.25 inches (22.86-23.49 centimeters) in circumference to meet Major League standards. Such uniformity did not exist in the early years of baseball's history. Balls were either homemade or custom-made by cobblers, tanners, or other small business owners, so the ball's size and weight varied.

At the turn of the century, the baseball had a round rubber core. This gave way in 1910 to the livelier cork-centered ball, which was then replaced around 1930 by a cushioned cork model that was more resilient (able to resume its original shape after bat abuse).

Baseball Materials

A baseball has three basic parts:

- the round cushioned cork center called a pill,

- the wool and poly/cotton yarns in the middle, and

- the cowhide covering on the outside.

A typical baseball.

The pill consists of a sphere made of a cork and rubber material (see fig. 6). This sphere is enclosed by two layers of rubber, a black inner layer and a red outer layer. The inner layer is made up of two hemispheric shells of black rubber that are joined by red rubber washers (a disk to make a tight seal).

There are four distinct layers of wool and poly/cotton windings that surround the pill in circles of varying thickness. The first winding is made of four-ply (four strands twisted together) gray woolen yarn, the second of three-ply white woolen yarn, the third of three-ply gray woolen yarn, and the fourth of white poly/cotton finishing yarn. The first layer is the thickest. When wrapped tightly around the pill, it brings the circumference of the unfinished ball to 7 3/4 inches (19.68 centimeters). The size increases to 8 3/16 inches (20.77 centimeters) after the second winding, 8 3/4 inches (22.22 centimeters) after the third, and 8 7/8 inches (22.52 centimeters) after the fourth.

Wool was chosen as the main material for the baseball's windings

A short supply of horses in 1974 prompted a switch from horsehide to cowhide covers.

Batter swinging at pitched baseball.

Unwind a baseball from the outside in and you'll find more than 300 yards of yarn fit tightly under that cowhide.

because its natural resiliency and "memory" allow it to compress when pressure is applied, then rapidly return to its original shape. This property makes it possible for the ball to keep its perfect roundness despite being hit repeatedly during a game. A poly/cotton blend was selected for the outer winding to provide added strength and reduce the risk of tears when the ball's cowhide cover is applied.

Number One Grade, full-grained cowhide is the choice for a baseball's outer cover. Midwest Holstein cattle are the preferred donors because their hides have a better grain and are cleaner and smoother than those of cattle in other areas. The cover of an official baseball must be white, and it is hand-stitched in place with waxed red thread.

The Manufacturing Process

Baseball production is a process of adding layers of material (rubber, fabric, and cowhide) around a sphere about the size of a cherry. These materials are placed around the small sphere in three distinct ways: the rubber is molded, the fabric is wound, and the cowhide is sewn. The placement of materials is done under carefully controlled conditions to ensure that consistent size, shape, and quality are maintained.

Molding rubber

1 Two hemispheric shells of black rubber, each approximately $5/32$ of an inch (.39 centimeter) thick, are molded (fit closely) to a rubberized cork sphere measuring $13/16$ of an inch (2.06 centimeters) in diameter. The small opening that separates these shells is sealed with red rubber (see top of fig. 6).

2 Next, a layer of red rubber roughly $3/32$ of an inch (.24 centimeter) thick is molded to the black rubber layer. The entire "pill" is then molded into a perfect circle weighing approximately $7/8$ of an ounce (24.80 grams) with a circumference of roughly $4\,1/8$ inches (10.48 centimeters). Once the pill has been molded, a thin layer of cement is applied to its surface to keep the first winding of wool yarn in place.

Winding fabric

3 Wool yarn that has been stored under controlled temperature and humidity conditions is wound around the pill. This is done by computerized winding machines that maintain a constant level of very high tension to eliminate "soft spots" and create a smooth surface. After each step in the winding process, the ball is weighed and measured by computer to assure that official size requirements are met.

The wool yarn is wound so tightly that it looks like thread when a baseball is dissected. Three layers of wool are wound around the baseball. The first is 121 yards (110.6 meters) of four-ply gray yarn; the second is 45 yards (41.13 meters) of three-ply white yarn; and the third, 53 yards (48.44 meters) of three-ply gray yarn.

4 Next comes a layer of 150 yards (137.1 meters) of fine poly/cotton finishing yarn wrapped around the ball to protect the wool yarn and hold it in place. The wound ball is then trimmed of any extra fabric and prepared for the cowhide cover by being dipped in glue.

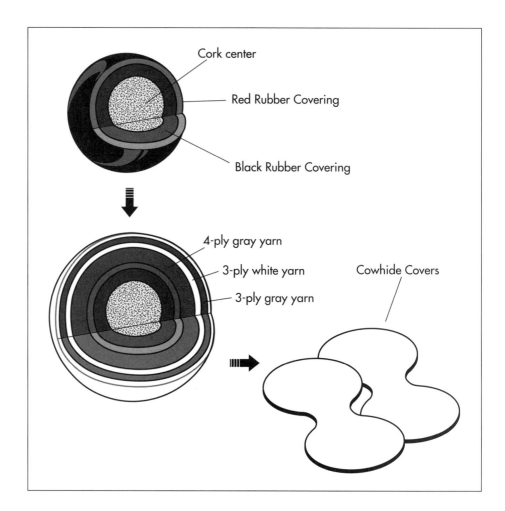

Fig. 6. Manufacturing a baseball involves molding two shells of black rubber to a rubberized cork. After a thin layer of red rubber is molded to the ball and a layer of cement is applied, three layers of multi-ply wool yarn are wound around the ball. A final layer of poly/cotton finishing yarn is next wrapped around the ball. Finally the cowhide cover is stapled to the ball and then stitched together.

Sewing hide

5 The cowhide covering is cut into two figure-8 patterns (see fig. 6). Each pattern covers half the wound ball. Before they are stitched to the ball, the covers are dampened to increase their elasticity. The insides of the covers also receive a coating of the same glue that was applied to the wound ball.

6 The two figure-8 coverings are stapled to the wound ball, then they are hand-sewn together using exactly 88 inches (223.52 centimeters) of waxed red thread. There are 108 stitches in the sewing process, with the first and last stitches completely hidden. An average of 13 to 14 minutes is required to stitch together a baseball cover (see fig. 7).

7 After the covers have been stitched, the staples are removed and the ball is inspected. The ball is then placed in a rolling machine for 15 seconds to level any raised stitches. The baseballs are then measured, weighed, and graded for appearance. Only acceptable baseballs are stamped with the manufacturer's trademark and league destination.

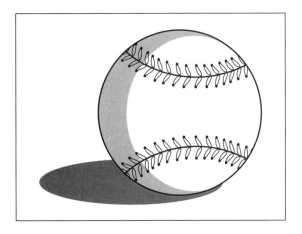

Fig. 7. A finished baseball, with 88 inches of waxed red thread holding two cowhide covering pieces together, weighs between 5 and 5.25 ounces and measures between 9 and 9.25 inches around.

Quality Control

A percentage of each shipment of baseballs is tested to measure Co-Efficient of Restitution (COR)—an indication of the resiliency of a baseball. The testing procedure is officially sanctioned by Major League Baseball.

The COR test involves shooting a baseball from an air cannon at a velocity (speed) of 85-feet-a-second (25.9-meters-a-second) at a wooden wall from a distance of eight feet (2.43 meters), then measuring the speed at which the ball bounces off the wall. Major League COR rules require that it must rebound at 54.6 percent of the initial velocity, plus or minus 3.2 percent.

That's not all. A baseball must also retain its round shape after being hit 200 times by a 65-pound (29.51 kilograms) force. As further proof of its strength, a baseball must distort less than 0.08 of an inch (.20 centimeter) after being pressed between two heavy iron blocks.

The Future is History

The size of baseballs and the materials used to make them are likely to remain unchanged in the foreseeable future. Also, few, if any, changes are expected in the process by which baseballs are manufactured.

Attempts to automate the process of sewing cowhide covers on baseballs have failed. Experiments with machines reveal two serious problems: first, they are unable to start or stop the stitching process without human help; and second, they are unable to vary the tension of their stitches, something that is essential if the two figure-8 coverings are to fit securely without tearing.

It is also likely that the controversy about juiced-up balls will continue as long as the game of baseball is played and fans seek an explanation for fluctuations in the homerun output of favorite teams and players.

WHERE TO LEARN MORE

Berler, Ron. *The Super Book of Baseball*. Time, 1991.

Gordon, John S. "The American Game," *American Heritage*. April 1991, pp. 19-20.

How Things Are Made. National Geographic Society, 1981.

Kluger, Jeffrey. "What's Behind the Home Run Boom?" *Discover*. April 1988, pp. 78-79.

Blue Jeans

The Casual Classic

In a world where fashion is notoriously fickle, blue jeans have been a wardrobe basic for more than a century. As fast as clothes styles change, rugged denim remains popular and in demand from year to year, season to season, even generation to generation, with only minor evolutions. The cloth may fade, but the fad never seems to fade away.

Blue jeans are casual pants made from strong yet comfortable denim cloth. They have long been a favorite sturdy work pant for farmers, sailors, miners, and cowboys. For the last 50 years students and young people have adopted jeans as an unofficial uniform, and smart designers have labeled them as trend-setting status symbols.

Denim has a long history. The name comes from serge de Nimes or serge (a strong, twill cloth) made in Nimes, France. Originally it was made from wool. During the 1700s, however, weavers added cotton to the cloth; later it was made from cotton alone. At first the tough stuff was used to make sails. Eventually some savvy Genovese (from Genoa, Italy) sailors decided the strong material would make great pants, or "genes" (the origin of "jeans").

Jeans were blue because denim was treated with a blue dye from the indigo plant. Indigo had been used as a dye since 2500 B.C. in Asia, Egypt, Greece, Rome, Britain, and Peru. Blue jean manufacturers imported indigo from India until the twentieth century when synthetic (artificial) indigo was developed.

Denim can be prewashed, stone washed, acid washed, bleached, faded, over-dyed, sandblasted, or torn. Designers have even tampered with their blues; denim is now available in many colors.

Two miners wearing their Levi's at the Last Chance Mine, Placer County, California, 1882.

Blue jeans as they're known today were invented in 1853 by Levi Strauss, a German immigrant. Strauss was a San Francisco merchant with extra bolts of blue denim in his storeroom. He noticed that miners who flocked to California looking for gold needed tough work pants. He designed and marketed denim pants as "Levi's," and within 10 years miners, farmers, and cowboys wore them daily.

Original Levi's didn't have rivets (metal fasteners) in their seams. A Russian immigrant tailor named Jacob Davis invented riveted pants for a miner who complained that simply stitched denim wasn't rugged enough to hold his tools. Strauss bought the idea from Davis in 1873 for $69, the price of a U.S. patent application (a patent gives an inventor the sole right to sell, make, or use his idea). Few other changes were made over the next century. Zippers replaced button flies in 1920 (although button flies have since made a fashion comeback).

Christopher Columbus's ships supposedly sported denim sails.

In 1937 rivets on the back of jeans were moved inside the pockets because of complaints from school boards that students' jean rivets scratched up their desks. Cowboys had the same concerns about their saddles being damaged, parents worried over family furniture, and car fenders were taking a beating. In the 1960s, rivets disappeared entirely from back pockets.

During the 1950s blue jeans became popular among teenagers. Manufacturers sold 150 million pairs worldwide in 1957. Ten years later U.S. customers alone purchased 200 million pairs. In 1977 Americans bought 500 million pairs. When jeans first caught on, fashion experts believed the low cost was responsible for their huge success. During the 1970s, howev-

Blue jeans hanging on the line to dry.

er, the price of blue jeans doubled, yet demand still exceeded supply. Sometimes manufacturers met the demand by selling irregulars; that is, slightly defective merchandise that would not normally be sold.

Although the demand for jeans actually decreased in the late 1970s, a brief surge occurred with the introduction of designer jeans to the market. Popular fashion designers around the world began marketing their own jean styles and charged top dollar for them. Manufacturers constantly seek ways to keep the demand for jeans high. They carefully analyze buying trends to design denims comfortable enough to suit everyone from babies to senior citizens.

Blue Jean Materials

True blue jeans are made out of 100 percent cotton, including the thread used to sew them. Polyester blends are available, but not as popular. The most common dye used is synthetic indigo. Rivets have been traditionally made of copper, but the zippers, snaps, and buttons are usually steel. Designers' labels are tags made of cloth, leather, or plastic, while some are embroidered on with cotton thread.

New on the fashion fabric market are eco-safe colored cottons. Scientist Sally Fox develops and grows natural cotton in soft greens and browns at her Arizona ranch. She hopes to someday develop yellows, reds, and grays—but never blue (that color chromosome just doesn't exist on cotton genes). Typically, cotton gets its color from a dye process. FoxFibre, her cotton trademark, has the extra advantage of being bleach and dye free— so their manufacture does not produce harmful by-products, nor does the color fade when washed.

The Manufacturing Process

Preparing the cotton yarn

1 There are several steps between ginned cotton (cotton after it has been picked from fields and processed) and cotton yarn. The incoming cotton is removed from tightly packed bales and inspected before undergoing a process known as carding (see fig. 8). In this process, the cotton is put through machines that contain brushes with bent wire teeth. These brushes, called cards, clean, untangle, straighten, and gather together cotton fibers. At this point, the fibers are called slivers.

2 Other machines join several slivers together, pulling and twisting them for added strength. Next, these sliver ropes are put on spinning machines that further twist and stretch the fibers to form yarn (see fig. 8).

Dyeing the yarn

3 Some cloths are woven (see step 5) and then dyed, but denim is usually dyed before being woven. Large balls of yarn, called ball warps, are dipped in synthetic indigo several times so that the dye covers the yarn in layers (see fig. 9). The multi-layers of indigo dye explain why blue jeans fade slightly with each washing. Although the exact chemicals used in the dyeing process remain trade secrets, it is known that a small amount of sulfur is added to stabilize the top or bottom layers of dye.

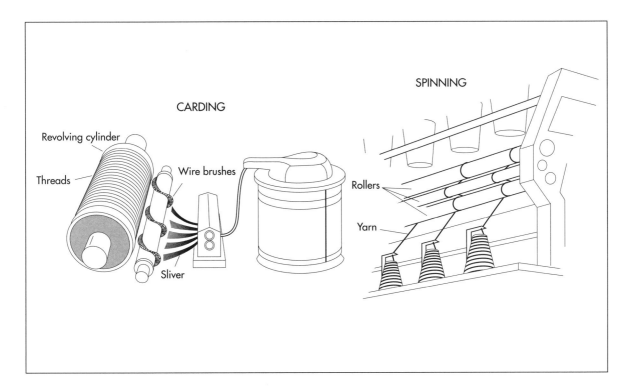

Fig. 8. The first two steps in blue jeans manufacture are carding and spinning.

4 The dyed yarn is then slashed, that is, coated with sizing (a starchy substance). Sizing makes the threads stronger and stiffer. Once this is completed, the dyed yarn threads are ready to be woven with undyed filling yarn threads.

Weaving the yarn

5 Next, the yarn is woven on large mechanical looms (see fig. 9). Denim is not 100 percent blue, since the blue-dyed threads forming the warp (long, vertical threads) are combined with white threads forming the weft (shorter, horizontal threads). Because the blue threads are packed more closely together than the white, the blue color dominates.

Mechanical looms use the same basic weaving procedure as a simple hand loom, but are much larger and faster. A modern "shuttle-less" loom (which uses a very small carrier instead of the traditional shuttle to weave

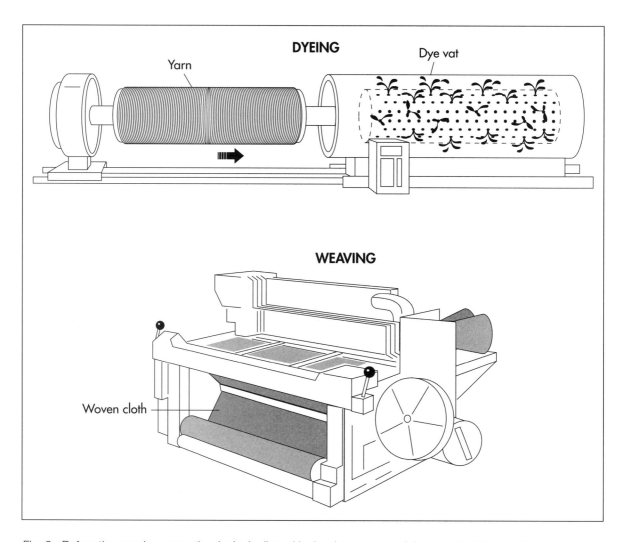

DYEING

Yarn

Dye vat

WEAVING

Woven cloth

Fig. 9. Before the yarn is woven, the denim is dipped in the dye vat several times so that the dye forms many layers.

the weft threads between the warp threads) may produce more than 3,000 yards of cloth in a single week. More than 1,000 yards of cloth may be rolled into a single huge bolt.

6 At this point denim is ready for finishing, a term referring to a variety of treatments applied to cloth after it is woven. The cloth is brushed to remove loose threads and lint and pinned to prevent it from twisting. The cloth may also be sanforized, or preshrunk. Sanforized denim should shrink no more than 3 percent after three washings.

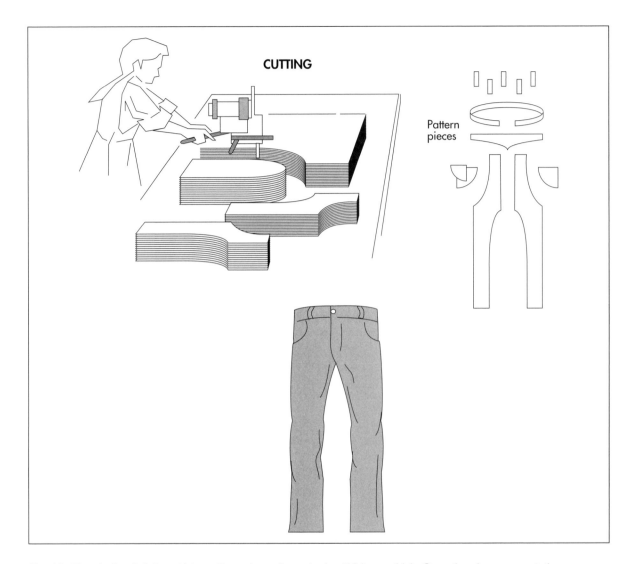

CUTTING

Pattern pieces

Fig. 10. The denim cloth is cut into pattern pieces from stacks 100 layers thick. Once the pieces are cut, they are sewn into completed pairs of blue jeans. Sewing is done in assembly-line fashion by workers using sewing machines.

Making the blue jeans

7 Once the design is selected, patterns are cut from heavy paper or cardboard (see fig. 10). Up to 80 different sizes are possible from one pattern. The pieces of denim are cut with high-speed cutting machines from stacks 100 layers thick. Excluding rivets, buttons, and zippers, a pair of blue jeans contains about 10 different pieces, including the pockets, leg panels, waistband, and belt loops.

8 Sewing comes next. Sewing is done in assembly-line fashion, with rows of workers operating industrial sewing machines. Each sewer is assigned a single job, such as making the back pockets.

First the pockets and belt loops are made. Next, one sewer attaches the pockets to the leg seams, another sews the leg seams together, and still another attaches the waistband. Then belt loops, buttons, and zippers are attached. Finally, rivets are stamped onto certain seams, and the maker's label is sewn in.

9 Some jeans are prewashed and/or stonewashed to change their appearance or texture. Prewashing means washing the jeans in industrial detergent for a short time to soften the denim. Abrasive (rough) stones are added to the wash for stonewashed or faded cloth. Small stones (one inch or less) cause an even fading, while large stones (four inches) highlight seams and pockets for an uneven color.

10 A completed pair of blue jeans is sent to a large pressing machine that steam irons the entire garment in about one minute. A size tag is punched into the material and the jeans are folded, stacked, and placed in boxes according to style, color, and size. Jeans are stored in a warehouse until they're packed in shipping cartons and sent by train or truck to a store.

By-Products/Waste

The manufacture of cloth involves a number of chemicals. Each step (dyeing, sanforizing, etc.) produces by-products (left over waste materials), most of which are biodegradable (decompose naturally, in a way which is harmless to the environment).

Some by-products of denim manufacture include pollutants (such as starch and dye). These waste products cannot be dumped into streams or lakes because they damage the water supply, plants, and animals. Manufacturers must follow government laws for disposal of waste.

Quality Control

Cotton is a popular natural fiber because it is strong and flexible. All bales of cotton are inspected by the denim manufacturer for the desired color, fiber length, and strength. Strength is measured by using a weight to pull on the cotton fiber. When the fiber breaks, the force used to break it is measured. The cotton's strength rating is calculated based on this weight.

Finished denim is carefully inspected for defects. Each defect is rated on a scale defined by the government. The scale assigns one point for very small flaws, and up to four points for major defects. Poor cloth can be sold as "damaged" if it is so labeled. Denim is also tested for durability and tendency to shrink. Samples of cloth are washed and dried several times to see how they wear.

Blue jeans are also inspected after they are sewn. If a problem can be corrected, the jeans are sent back for re-sewing and another inspection. Buttons are checked for size match to buttonholes. Snaps, metal buttons, and rivets are checked for strength and rust-resistance. Zippers must be strong enough to handle the pressures of heavy cloth, so sample zippers are tested with hundreds of openings and closings.

Jeans of the Future

Although blue jeans have remained basically the same since they were first designed, they've always been versatile enough to meet market demands. Jeans have been favorites with miners, farmers, cowboys, and students. If movies can deliver a fashion forecast, their appeal may last for another generation. Futuristic yet familiar "Levi's" were worn by space travelers in the movie *Star Trek V.*

WHERE TO LEARN MORE

Adkins, Jan. "The Evolution of Jeans: American History 501," *Mother Earth News.* July/August 1990, pp. 60-63.

"Blue Jeans," *Consumer Reports.* July 1991, pp. 456-61.

Caney, Steven. *Invention Book.* Workman Publishing Company, 1985.

Finlayson, Iain. *Denim.* Simon and Schuster, 1990.

Panati, Charles. *Extraordinary Origins of Everyday Things.* Harper & Row, 1987.

Reader's Digest: How in the World? Reader's Digest, 1990.

Book

Food for Thought

Books can be defined as written documents of at least 49 pages that communicate thoughts, ideas, or information. Throughout the ages, books have changed dramatically, assuming many different forms. The evolution of the book is related to the growth of communication and the ever-increasing demand for information.

The first known written documents were the clay tablet of Mesopotamia and the papyrus roll (sheets made from reed plants placed side by side then rolled up in long scrolls) of Egypt. Examples of both date back as early as 3000 B.C. Chinese books made of wood or bamboo strips bound together with cords date back to 1300 B.C.

Modern book production resulted from the invention of the printing press by Johann Gutenberg of Germany. Gutenberg and his partners, Johann Fust and Peter Schoffer, printed a Latin Bible (which means "the book") in 1456, using a hand printing press with movable lead type. Each individual letter of early hand-set type was designed to resemble script or hand lettering. Thus, the first books printed in Europe appeared much like books produced by scribes (people who wrote books by hand). Books printed in the fifteenth century are now called incunabula, a term derived from the Latin word for cradle.

The first books were rare, costly, and prized possessions. Just imagine scribes of the fifteenth century struggling by candlelight to hand print each page. Once the printing press and movable type mechanized the book production process, books became more affordable and available.

Typesetters at work in 1860.

By the nineteenth century, however, the demand for books could not be met quickly enough by the process of hand printing.

Printers developed larger presses to accommodate larger sheets of paper and/or the newly invented continuous rolls of paper. These improvements speeded production. During the mid-1800s further progress included the invention of the papermaking machine (1820s), binding machinery (1860), and the cylinder press (1840s). Later, the linotype (1884) cast type by line rather than by individual letter.

Book production in America and throughout the industrialized world flourished and expanded during the twentieth century. Important advances in printing, such as the introduction of the offset printing press (see fig. 12) and computerized typesetting (see fig. 11), made mass production more economical.

The development of the paperback book in the 1940s was a less expensive alternative to the traditional hardback book and also made books more available to the public. While the invention of radio and tele-

Machines can't produce pop-up books. The life-like, movable pictures are printed on paper then hand-made on manual assembly lines where workers sit at long tables to hand-cut, fold, and glue them onto pages. "Casing in" (attaching the book to its cover) is also done by hand since these books cannot be pressed.

vision reduced the need to read in general, books remain the primary source of knowledge throughout most of the world.

Book Materials

Books are made from a variety of different coated and uncoated papers that differ in weight and size. In addition, different color inks may be used. While front and back covers are generally made from a heavier type of paper, they also vary in terms of weight. For example, hardback books have a durable cardboard cover while paperback books are made from a thinner paper. Usually covers are coated with different colors or designs.

Since the nineteenth century, book production has involved the use of sophisticated machinery, including typesetting machines, a web (continuous) or sheet-fed printing press, and book binding machines.

Design Options

The process of designing a book is ongoing throughout the stages of production. First, the author meets with an editor and book agent to consider elements of design that relate to the purpose of the book, and the desired approach to the subject matter. They decide whether illustrations should be used and choose the placement and style of chapter headings. Careful attention is given to the intended audience and accepted editorial standards when making those decisions.

Other design considerations include whether a book should have a preface, a foreword, a glossary to define specific terms, an index to reference key words and concepts, and an appendix (listing at the end) of supplementary (related) material.

Once the book manuscript (author's hand-written or typed version before publication) is written, editors and authors refine it to achieve a final, edited version (correct grammar, spelling, meanings, etc.). In most cases, this involves a process of reviewing, rewriting, editing, proofreading, revising, and final approval. After such factors are completed, editors and art directors will determine the following features:

- page size and style,

- typeface size and style,
- the type and weight of paper for the text and cover,
- use of color,
- presentation of visuals/illustrations in the text, if needed,
- cover art or illustrations.

The Manufacturing Process

After the book is written and design elements are agreed upon, production can begin. The first stage is typesetting, in which actual text is converted into the appropriate typeface style (known as font) and size (known as point size).

After the typeset version of the book has been reviewed and any necessary changes made, it is ready for printing and binding. This is when the actual pages are printed and bound together with the cover, resulting in a finished book (see fig. 13). The typesetting and printing are often not done by the publisher, but by typesetters and printers.

Hard cover and soft cover books

Typesetting

1 First, the manuscript is converted into the desired font and point size. If the manuscript has not been completed on a computer, it must be typed into a computer by the typesetter. (see fig. 11). If it is already in electronic form, however, the typesetter simply has to make programming changes to convert the manuscript into the proper style. The result is generally (but not always; see step #3) a galley of the text. A galley manuscript consists of long pages of text in a single column, as wide as it will appear on the book pages. The galley includes the proper typeface, but the proper pagination (division into pages) still must be worked out.

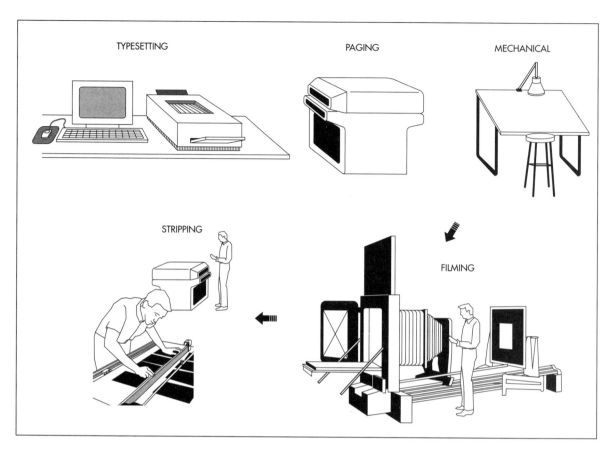

Fig. 11. The first step in book production is typesetting. Once typeset, the camera-ready copy is sent to a printer. The printer then photographs the pages to produce page negatives, which are then stripped and made into blueprints.

2 Galleys are then proofread and checked for errors by the publisher. This stage is particularly important if the manuscript has been typeset (typed) from a hard copy of the text. If the manuscript was typeset from a computer disk, most of the errors should have already been corrected during a review of the manuscript. The single-column format of galleys makes proofreading easier.

Pages and mechanical

3 After galleys are thoroughly proofed and edited, pages are produced. An exact layout of typeset pages is usually printed on standard typing paper; pages are also reviewed for accuracy by the pub-

lisher. Some books skip the galley stage and go directly to pages. Once any necessary changes have been made, the typesetter then produces a mechanical (camera copy) of the typed pages. The mechanical is printed on high-quality paper suitable for filming, or photographing, the first stage in the printing process.

Filming

4 The typeset mechanical copy now goes to the printer and binder. First, each text page, including line drawings, is photographed (or shot) using a large camera to produce page negatives or film transparencies (see fig. 11). These negatives are the opposite of what will actually print. In other words, the text and photos will appear backward in negative form. Negatives are then checked to make sure there are no blemishes or spots.

While printed words and line drawings are all one shade of black, photographs have many shades from palest gray to deepest black and must be filmed using a special process to maintain these shades. The process converts the shades into black and white dots—very light areas have many dots, while darker areas have fewer dots. The converted photographs are known as halftones.

If the book will have more than one color of ink, a separate negative for each color is made. For color photos, for instance, four negatives are generally used: cyan (greenish-blue), magenta (deep purplish-red), yellow, and black. For this reason, books with color will have negative overlays (one negative overlay for each color, so that when one is laid over, or combined with another, the blended colors will result in a complete, full-color picture). Because of the added overlays, a book printed in more than one color involves extra preparation and cost.

Stripping

5 The negatives are then taped or "stripped" into their proper place onto a large flat sheet called a goldenrod or a flat (see fig. 11). Each flat holds 32 or 64 pages, and enough flats are used to equal the number of pages in the book. Strippers examine each finished flat on a lineup table to ensure that text and pictures are properly lined up and in correct order.

Some of the pages are placed upside down because the finished paper version of each flat will be folded several times. Once the flat is folded, the 32 or 64 pages will be in the proper order. This placement method is known as imposition. To make this process easier, the lineup tables are equipped with a fluorescent light that shines up through the negatives, so it is easier for the stripper to read and align the text.

Blueprints

6 To make sure the book is progressing properly, a proof of each flat is made by shining ultraviolet light through the negatives to expose their images onto a special light-sensitive paper. The resulting pages are called blueprints (or silverprints, bluelines, or dyluxes) because the paper and ink are blue or silver in appearance. The blueprints are then checked carefully by the publisher. If an editor or art director finds an error on a blueprint or decides to make a change, the page in question has to be rephotographed. The new negative will then be stripped onto the flat.

Plate making

7 After final approval, each flat is photographed, with the negatives being exposed onto (or "burned" onto) a thin sheet of aluminum called a plate. The sections of the plates that contain text and illustrations are then treated with a chemical that attracts ink, thereby ensuring that the text and illustrations will print when on press.

Printing

8 The plates are then sent to press (see fig. 12). If printing in only one color, each plate will require only one pass through the press. If printing more than one color, an extra pass will be needed for each color. For example, if two colors are used, the paper is fed through the press twice.

There are three main printing processes used in book production: offset lithography (transfer of ink from a hard surface), letterpress (from a raised ink surface), and gravure (with etched plates or cylinders). The process used depends less on quality differences than on economic factors such as availability of machines, number of books being printed (the print run), and the speed of delivery. Presses are either sheet-fed (single sheets of paper are fed through) or web-fed (huge rolls of paper are unwound and run through).

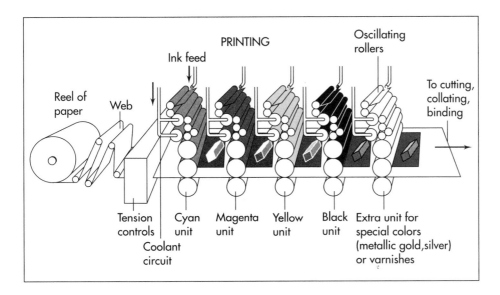

Fig. 12. Printing is often done on an offset lithography printing press, in which the paper is fed through rolls that are exposed to the proper ink. If colored ink is necessary, either for text or for photographs, each of the four major colors is offset onto its own set of rollers.

Binding

9 After the sheets are printed and dry, they are delivered to the bindery (see fig. 13). Here, the flats are folded and collated (arranged in correct numerical order) into book signatures (properly folded 32- or 64-page sections) that are then bound in proper sequence. All of these functions are automated (done by machine).

10 Book binding also involves sewing the signatures together, gluing the spine (hinged back), inserting a lining into the spine for reinforcement, and trimming the edges. The amount and type of binding depends on the type of book (paperback or hardback) and its size. In the final step, the book is "cased in," or enclosed in a cover.

Quality Control

Print shops conduct a number of periodic quality checks. In addition to checking blueprints for accuracy, printers will pull a press proof, or sample, before the print run is begun. If certain areas of the proof are too light or too dark, adjustments to the press are made.

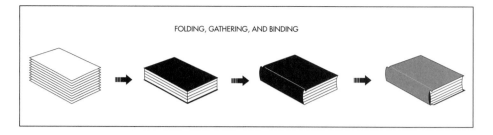

Fig. 13. After printing, the sections of the book—in 32- or 64-page pieces—are folded properly, sewn together, and bound with the book jacket or cover.

After the book signatures are sewn together, the print shop will spot-check them to make sure they have been folded and sewn correctly. They will also check to see if the book covers are properly bound to prevent the books from coming apart when used.

Some of the instruments used to control quality include densitometers and colorimeters, both of which evaluate color printing processes; paper hygroscopes, which measure the moisture balance of paper against the humidity of printing rooms; and inkometers, which measure the quality of the ink to be used in printing.

The Future

Book production has changed little since the early twentieth century, with the exception of typesetting. Typesetting machines have been standard equipment in print shops and businesses since 1900, but desktop publishing on microcomputers has become a less expensive alternative. With the proper typesetting software and a laser printer, users can produce text, insert graphics, and create layouts and page designs that are as sophisticated as those produced by traditional methods. As a result, authors, publishers, print shops, and just about every other business have been able to set type and perform page layout and design on their own microcomputers. Depending on the quality of the laser printer, users can create type that a printer can use to shoot a negative. Such type is referred to as camera-ready.

Many authors, publishers, and design shops now have their own desktop publishing equipment, allowing them to give printers camera-ready copy. If they do not have laser printers with fine enough print quality, they can simply give the printer the book in disk form and have the printer run the type out on a laser printer. Either way, desktop publishing gives the user more design control and cuts down on production costs. As more people gain access to such systems, book publication and publishing in general will see more widespread use of desktop publishing in the future.

WHERE TO LEARN MORE

Library of Science Technology. Marshall Cavendish Corporation, 1989.

Macaulay, David. *The Way Things Work*. Houghton Mifflin Company, 1988.

Perrins. *How Paper Is Made*. Facts on File, 1986.

The Visual Dictionary of Everyday Things. Dorling Kindersley, 1991.

Walters, Sarah. *How Newspapers Are Made*. Facts on File, 1989.

Bulletproof Vest

Some vest manufacturers and wearers prefer the term bullet resistant vest because the wearer is not totally safe from bullets.

Suit Yourself

Bulletproof vests are modern-day light armor designed to protect the wearer's vital organs from injury caused by firearms. Over the centuries, many different cultures developed body armor for use during combat. Cavemen cushioned themselves against the blows of hostile clubs with layers of animal fur. Mycenaeans (from the ancient Greek city of Mycenae) of the sixteenth century B.C. and Persians and Greeks around the fifth century B.C. used up to fourteen layers of linen, while Micronesians (from islands in the West Pacific Ocean) found suits of woven coconut palm fiber useful until the nineteenth century.

The Chinese—as early as the eleventh century B.C.—wore rhinoceros skin in five to seven layers, and North American Shoshone Indians developed jackets of several layers of hide that were glued or sewn together. Quilted armor was available in Central America before Hernando Cortés arrived to attack the Aztecs during the early 1500s. The English wore quilted armor in the seventeenth century, and it was used in India until the nineteenth century.

Hard Wear vs. Soft Wear

Mail armor was made of linked rings or wires of iron, steel, or brass and was developed as early as 400 B.C. near the Ukrainian city of Kiev. Conquering soldiers of the Roman Empire wore mail shirts, which remained the main piece of armor in Europe until the fourteenth century. Japan, India, Persia, Sudan, and Nigeria also developed mail armor.

Scale armor, overlapping scales of metal, horn, bone, leather, or scales from an appropriately scaled animal (such as the scaly anteater), was used throughout the Eastern Hemisphere from about 1600 B.C. until modern times. Sometimes, as in China, the scales were sewn into cloth pockets.

Twelfth century Europeans armed themselves with heavy coats of metal plates, but the ultimate in protection was the familiar full-plate suit of armor worn by knights in the 1500s and 1600s. Some sol-

This type of armor, tilting armor, was used for sport (jousting) only.

diers even covered their horses with armor before venturing into battle, a practice which undoubtedly slowed their progress.

Brigandine armor—sleeveless, quilted jackets—was more flexible and practical. It consisted of small rectangular iron or steel plates bolted onto leather strips that overlapped like roof tiles. The result was a relatively light, flexible jacket. Many consider brigandine armor the forerunner of today's bulletproof vests. The Chinese and Koreans had similar armor around A.D. 700, and during the fourteenth century in Europe, it was the common form of body armor. One piece of breastplate within a cover became the norm after 1360, and Europeans preferred short brigandine coats with plates that were tied into place until 1600.

With the introduction of firearms (guns), armor crafts workers at first tried to reinforce the cuirass, or torso cover, with thicker steel plates and a

Russian scientists prepare to test new bulletproof gear designed for special forces in Moscow, 1994.

second heavy plate over the breastplate. Usually though, the heavy, cumbersome armor was abandoned wherever firearms came into military use.

Experiments to develop an armor more effective against gunfire continued, especially during the American Civil War, World War I, and World War II. Not until the plastics revolution of the 1940s did really effective bulletproof vests become available to law enforcement, military personnel, and others. These early vests were made of a sturdy nylon and supplemented by plates of fiberglass, steel, ceramic, and titanium (a metallic element often used in aircraft because of its strength and light weight). Combinations of ceramic and fiberglass proved the most effective.

In 1965, Stephanie Kwolek, a chemist at E. I. du Pont de Nemours & Company (a chemical company), invented Kevlar, the trademark name for poly-para-phenylene terephthalamide, a liquid polymer (a substance formed by the union of many molecules) that can be spun into a fiber and woven into cloth.

Originally, Kevlar was developed for use in tires, and later for such diverse products as ropes, gaskets (seals used between machine parts to prevent leaks), and various parts for planes and boats. In 1971, Lester Shubin of the National Institute of Law Enforcement and Criminal Justice suggested its use to replace the bulky nylon in bulletproof vests. Kevlar has been the standard material since.

In 1989 Allied Signal developed a competitor for Kevlar and called it Spectra. Originally used for sail cloth, the polyethylene fiber is now used to make lighter, yet stronger, nonwoven material for use in bulletproof vests alongside the traditional Kevlar.

Raw Materials

A bulletproof vest consists of a panel, a vest-shaped sheet of advanced plastics that is composed of many layers of either Kevlar, Spectra Shield, or, in other countries, Twaron (similar to Kevlar) or Bynema (similar to Spectra). The layers of woven Kevlar are sewn together using Kevlar thread, while the nonwoven Spectra Shield is coated and bonded (joined securely) with resins (a sticky substance produced by certain plants and trees) and then sealed between two sheets of polyethylene film.

The panel provides protection but not much comfort. It is placed inside of a fabric shell that is usually made from a polyester/cotton blend or nylon. The side of the shell facing the body is usually made more comfortable by sewing a sheet of some absorbent material such as Kumax onto it. A bulletproof vest may also have nylon padding for extra protection. Vests intended to be worn in especially dangerous situations have built-in pouches to hold plates made from either metal or ceramic bonded to fiberglass. Such vests can also provide protection in car accidents or from knives.

Various devices are used to strap the vests on. Sometimes the sides are connected with elastic webbing. Usually, though, they are secured with straps of either cloth or elastic, with metallic buckles or velcro closures (see fig. 15).

The Manufacturing Process

Some bulletproof vests are custom-made to meet the specific protection needs and size of the user. Most, however, meet standard protection regulations, have standard clothing industry sizes (such as 38 long, 32 short), and are sold in quantity.

The increase of violent crime in cities has prompted the design of protective clothing for schoolchildren and businesspeople.

Making the panel cloth

1 To make Kevlar, the polymer poly-para-phenylene terephthalamide must first be produced in the laboratory. This is done through a process known as polymerization, which involves combining small molecules to make larger ones. The resultant crystalline liquid with polymers in the shape of rods is then extruded (pushed out) through a spinneret (a small metal plate full of tiny holes that looks like a shower head) to form Kevlar yarn (see fig. 14). The Kevlar fiber then passes through a cooling bath to harden. After being sprayed with water, the synthetic fiber is wound onto rolls. The fibers are then twisted together to make a yarn

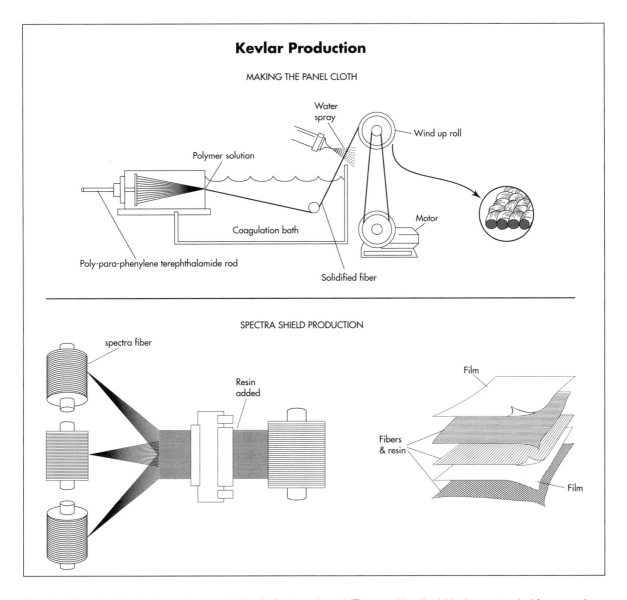

Kevlar Production

MAKING THE PANEL CLOTH

Water spray

Wind up roll

Polymer solution

Poly-para-phenylene terephthalamide rod

Coagulation bath

Solidified fiber

Motor

SPECTRA SHIELD PRODUCTION

spectra fiber

Resin added

Film

Fibers & resin

Film

Fig. 14. To make Kevlar, the polymer solution is first produced. The resulting liquid is then extruded from a spinneret, cooled with water, stretched on rollers, and wound into cloth.

suitable for weaving. To make Kevlar cloth, the yarns are woven in the simplest pattern, plain or tabby weave, which is merely the over and under pattern of interlacing threads.

Spectra Shield is not woven but rather spun into fibers that are then laid parallel to each other. The fibers are coated with resin and layered to form the cloth.

2 Unlike Kevlar, the Spectra used in bulletproof vests is usually not woven. Instead, the strong polyethylene polymer filaments are spun into fibers that are then laid parallel to each other (see fig. 14). Resin is used to coat the fibers, sealing them together to form a sheet of Spectra cloth. Two sheets of this cloth are then placed at right angles to one another and again bonded, forming a nonwoven fabric that is sandwiched between two sheets of polyethylene film. The vest shape is then cut from the material.

Cutting the panels

3 Kevlar cloth is sent in large rolls to the bulletproof vest manufacturer. The fabric is unrolled onto a cutting table that must be long enough to allow several panels to be cut out at a time; sometimes it can be as long as 32.79 yards (30 meters). As many layers of the material as needed (as few as eight layers, or as many as 25, depending on the level of protection desired) are laid out on the cutting table.

4 A cut sheet, similar to pattern pieces used for home sewing, is then placed on the layers of cloth. For maximum use of the material, some manufacturers use computer graphics systems to determine the best placement of the cut sheets.

5 Workers use a hand-held machine that performs like a jigsaw except that instead of a cutting wire it has a 5.91-inch (15-centimeter) cutting wheel similar to that on the end of a pizza cutter (see fig. 15). They cut around the sheets to form panels, which are then placed in precise stacks.

Sewing the panels

6 While Spectra Shield generally does not require sewing, as its panels are usually just cut and stacked in layers that go into tight fitting pouches in the vest, a bulletproof vest made from Kevlar can be either quilt-stitched or box-stitched. Quilt-stitching forms small diamonds of cloth separated by stitching, whereas box stitching forms a large

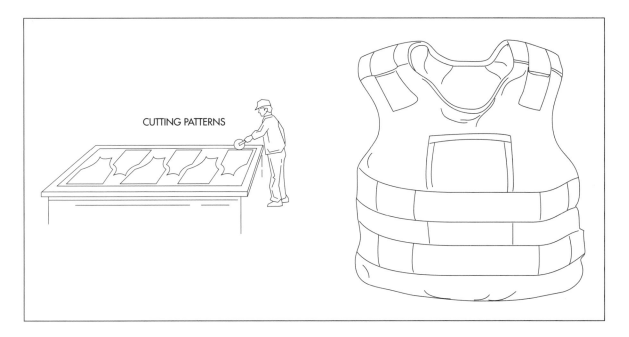

CUTTING PATTERNS

Fig. 15. After the cloth is made, it must be cut into the proper pattern pieces. These pieces are then sewn together with accessories (such as straps) to form the finished vest.

single box in the middle of the vest. Quilt-stitching requires more labor but provides a stiff panel that is hard to shift away from vulnerable areas. Box-stitching, on the other hand, is fast and easy and allows free movement of the vest.

7 To sew the layers together, workers place a stencil on top of the layers and rub chalk on the exposed areas of the panel, making a dotted line on the cloth. A sewer then stitches the layers together, following the chalk line. Next, a size label is sewn onto the panel.

Finishing the vest

8 The shells for the panels are sewn together in the same factory using standard industrial sewing machines and standard sewing practices. The panels are then slipped inside the shells, and the accessories—such as the straps—are sewn on (see fig. 15). The finished bulletproof vest is boxed and shipped to the customer.

A man strapping on a bulletproof vest.

*For police use,
the general rule
suggested by
experts is to
purchase a vest
that protects
against the type
of firearm the
officer normally
carries.*

Quality Control

Bulletproof vests undergo many of the same tests a regular piece of clothing does. The fiber manufacturer tests the fiber and yarn tensile strength (resistance to a tearing force), and the fabric weavers test the strength of the cloth. Nonwoven Spectra is also tested for tensile strength by the manufacturer. Vest manufacturers test the panel material (whether Kevlar or Spectra) for strength, and production quality control requires that trained observers inspect the vests after the panels are sewn and the vests completed.

Bulletproof vests, unlike regular clothing, must undergo stringent (rigid, strict) protection testing as required by the National Institute of Justice (NIJ). Not all bulletproof vests are alike. Some protect against lead bullets at low velocity (speed), while others protect against full metal jacketed bullets at high velocity.

Testing a vest, wet or dry, involves wrapping it around a modeling clay dummy. A firearm of the correct type with a bullet of the correct type is then shot at a velocity suitable for the classification of the vest. Each shot should be three inches (7.6 centimeters) away from the edge of the vest and almost two inches (five centimeters) away from previous shots. Six shots are fired, two at a 30-degree angle of incidence (angle formed by the path of a bullet and a perpendicular line to the surface of the vest), and four at a 0-degree angle of incidence. One shot should fall on a seam.

This method of shooting forms a wide triangle of bullet holes. The vest is then turned upside down and shot the same way, this time making a narrow triangle of bullet holes. To pass the test, the clay dummy should have no holes or pieces of vest or bullet in it. Though the bullet will leave a dent, it should be no deeper than 1.7 inches (4.4 centimeters).

When a vest passes inspection, the model number is certified and the manufacturer can then make exact duplicates of the vest. After the vest has been tested, it is placed in an archive (a place where evidence or information is stored) so that in the future, vests with the same model number can be easily checked against the prototype (original).

Field testing is not practical for bulletproof vests, but in a sense, wearers (such as police officers) test them everyday. Studies of wounded police officers have shown that bulletproof vests save hundreds of lives each year.

Bulletproof vests are tested both wet and dry. This is done because the fibers used to make vests perform differently when wet.

WHERE TO LEARN MORE

Free, John. "Lightweight Armor," *Popular Science*. June 1989, p. 30.

Tarassuk, Leonid, and Claude Blair, eds. *The Complete Encyclopedia of Arms and Weapons*. Simon and Schuster, 1979.

The Visual Dictionary of Military Uniforms. Dorling Kindersley, 1992.

Cheese

Curds and Whey

People have enjoyed cheese for more than 8,000 years. Long before Little Miss Muffet sat on her tuffet tasting her curds and whey, people knew that milk was good for more than just drinking. With little or no effort, farmers turned the white stuff into a chewy, tasty treat loaded with calcium and protein. Nutrition aside, cheese flavors everything from nachos to popcorn.

The French are the leading lovers of cheese. They produce about 750 varieties of cheese and consume about 50 pounds per person per year. Americans eat some 25 pounds per person per year.

Cheese is a solid food made from the milk of mammals. Around 10,000 B.C., when people began to domesticate milk-producing animals, they discovered that milk separates into curds (soft lumps) and whey (white, watery fluid). Protein-filled curds are the main ingredient of cheese. Nearly every country and culture has developed its own methods for producing cheese, so consumers can now choose from among nearly 2,000 varieties.

The first cheeses were simply salted white curds drained of whey, similar to today's cottage cheese. Farmers learned that if they left milk to sit, it would eventually separate naturally into curds and whey. The next step in cheese production was to develop a way to speed up the natural separation. This was achieved by adding rennet (an enzyme or protein found in a calf's stomach) or some other acid-like substance.

By A.D. 100 cheese makers learned how to press, ripen, and cure fresh cheeses, thereby creating a product that could be stored for long periods. Its popularity grew, and for the next thousand years or so, different regions developed different cheese types depending on local ingredients and methods used.

Just a sampling of the many types of cheese available to cheese lovers.

The next significant step to affect the manufacture of cheese occurred in the 1860s when scientist Louis Pasteur introduced his new process of sterilization. Pasteurization, as it came to be known, involved heating milk to kill harmful germs without changing its basic chemical structure. Today most cheese is made from pasteurized milk.

The simplest way to keep cheese from spoiling was to age it. Aged cheese was popular because it lasted a long time in home kitchens. In the 1300s, the Dutch began to seal the cheeses they exported in hard rinds (coatings or covers of wax or bacteria) to keep the product fresh.

The next cheese breakthrough came from Switzerland in the 1800s. The Swiss were the first to process cheese. Frustrated by cheese spoilage in the days before refrigeration, they developed a method of grinding old cheese, adding filler ingredients, and heating the mixture. This produced a sterile, uniform, long-lasting product. Another advantage of processing cheese was that it permitted cheese makers to recycle edible but second-grade cheeses into a popular product.

It takes one gallon of milk to make one pound of soft cheese, and five quarts for a pound of hard cheese.

In the past most people considered cheese a specialty food, produced in private homes for family members. However, with new methods of mass production, both the supply and demand for cheese have increased. In 1955, 13 percent of milk was made into cheese. By 1984 this had grown to 31 percent and continues to increase. Processed cheese is now widely available, and can be purchased in slices, spreads, and soft, easily poured sauces.

Despite the fact that most cheese is now made in large, modern factories, a majority are still made using the old-fashioned, natural methods. In fact "farmhouse" cheeses have made a comeback in recent years. Many Americans now own their own small cheese-making businesses, and their products are very popular.

Cheese Ingredients and Materials

Cheese is made from milk. Its flavor, color, and consistency are determined by the way it is made as well as its source. Most cheese comes from the milk of cows or goats, but cheese can be made from the milk of buffalo, sheep, camels, yaks, llamas, or reindeer. Some cheese makers even experiment with milk mixed from several sources.

Various ingredients, some rather surprising, may be added to enhance the flavor and color of cheese. The great cheeses of the world may acquire their flavor from bacterial molds that are sometimes added as part of the manufacturing process. Cheese makers who wish to avoid rennet may cause bacterial growth, which is necessary for curdling, by using unpasteurized milk or other methods. Cheeses may also be salted or dyed, usually with annatto an orange coloring made from carrot juice or the pulp of a tropical tree.

Processed cheese makers have created some unusual flavors and textures by combining several types of natural cheese and adding salt, cream, whey, water, and oil. The taste of processed cheese is also affected by preservatives, gelatins, thickeners, and sweeteners. Some popular flavor-enhancers include paprika, pepper, chives, onions, cumin, caraway seeds, jalapeño peppers, hazelnuts, raisins, wine, mushrooms, sage, and bacon. Cheese can also be smoked to preserve it and give it a distinctive flavor.

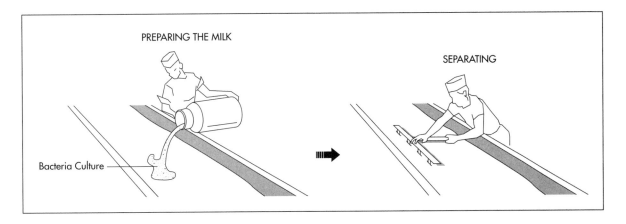

Fig. 16. In a typical cheese-making operation, the first step is preparing the milk. Next, the curds must be separated from the whey. As the whey separates, it is drained.

The Manufacturing Process

Although cheese making is a simple process, it involves many factors. Numerous varieties of cheese exist because ending the process at different stages can produce different cheeses. Various additives and methods will affect flavor. It is a delicate process. Attempts to duplicate the success of an old cheese factory failed because the proper bacteria wouldn't grow at the new factory.

Preparing the milk

1. Small cheese factories accept either morning milk (which is richer), evening milk, or both. Because it is generally purchased from small dairies that don't pasteurize, this milk contains the bacteria necessary to produce lactic acid, one of the ingredients that triggers curdling. Cheese makers let milk sit until enough lactic acid forms to begin producing the type of cheese they're making, and depending on the type being produced, cheese makers may then heat the ripening milk. This process differs slightly at large cheese factories, which use pasteurized milk and must add a culture of bacteria to produce lactic acid (see fig. 16).

Separating the curds from the whey

2. The next step is to add animal or vegetable rennet to the milk for fast separation into curds and whey. Once formed, the curds are cut both vertically and horizontally with knives (see fig. 16). In large

factories, huge vats of curdled milk are cut vertically using sharp, multi-bladed, wire knives that look like oven racks. The same machine then turns the curds and slices them horizontally. If the cutting is done by hand, the curds are cut both ways using a large two-handled knife. Soft cheeses are cut into big chunks, while hard cheeses are cut into tiny chunks. After cutting, the curds may be heated to hurry separation from whey or left alone. When separation is complete, the whey is drained off.

Pressing the curds

3 Moisture must then be extracted from the curds, although the amount removed depends on the type of cheese. For soft, high-moisture cheeses, draining is enough (see fig. 17). Drier, harder types require the curds to be cut, heated, and/or filtered to get rid of excess moisture. If the curds need to be aged, they are then put into molds where they are pressed into the proper shape and size. Soft cheeses such as cottage cheese are not aged (and must be eaten rather quickly since they have a shorter shelf life.)

Aging the cheese

4 At this stage the cheese may have a flavoring mold added, washed in brine (salty water used for preserving), or wrapped in cloth or hay. Then the cheese is aged in a controlled environment at just the right temperature and humidity (see fig. 17). Some cheeses are aged for a month, some for up to several years. Aging sharpens the flavor. For example, cheddar aged more than two years is labeled extra sharp.

Wrapping natural cheese

5 Some cheeses develop a rind (hard outer covering) naturally, as their surfaces dry. Other rinds form from the growth of bacteria that has been sprayed on the surface of the cheese. Still other cheeses are washed to encourage bacterial growth. In place of or in addition to rinds, cheeses can be sealed in cloth or wax. Cheese that is packaged for sale in distant countries may be heavily salted for export or sealed in plastic or foil.

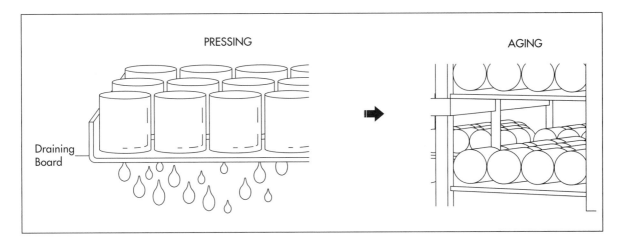

Fig. 17. The curds are then pressed into molds, if necessary, to help drain moisture, and aged for the proper amount of time. Some cheeses are aged for a month, others for several years.

Making and wrapping processed cheese

6 Edible yet inferior cheeses can be saved and made into processed cheese. Cheeses such as Emmental (commonly called Swiss), Gruyère (similar to Swiss), Colby, or cheddar are cut up and very finely ground. The resulting powder is mixed with water to form a paste, and other ingredients such as salt, fillers, preservatives, and flavorings are added. The mixture is then heated. While still warm and soft, the cheese paste is pushed out into long ribbon shapes, then sliced. The small sheets of cheese are then wrapped by machine in plastic or foil.

Quality Control

Cheese making is not an easily regulated, scientific process. Developing a single set of standards for cheese is difficult because each variety has its own range of characteristics. One cheese controversy centers around whether or not to use pasteurized milk. Some believe elimination of bacteria and germs makes a healthier product. Others say pasteurization spoils the flavor added by certain harmless bacteria.

Regulations exist so that consumers can buy authentic cheese easily. A cheese labeled "Roquefort" is guaranteed by law to have been manufactured in France and ripened in certain caves there. This guarantee has existed since 1411. Great care is taken to insure that the raw materials for cheese are of the highest quality and meet strict health standards.

Penicillium roqueforti is a bluish mold used to make blue (or bleu) cheeses such as the Roquefort cheese above.

Cheese is also graded on flavor, aroma, body, texture, color, appearance, and finish. Inspectors test a batch of cheese by taking samples from the center, sides, and middle. The inspector looks for flaws in texture, rubs it to determine body (or consistency), smells it, and tastes it. Cheese is usually given points for each of these characteristics.

Processed cheese is also subject to legal standards. Processed American cheese must contain at least 90 percent real cheese. Products labeled "cheese food" or "cheese spread" must be 51 percent cheese. Water and gums are added to make them spreadable. "Cheese products" and "imitation cheese" are not regulated for specific amounts of cheese, and cheese is not their main ingredient. In general, good processed cheese should have a nice cheesy flavor, be smooth but not rubbery, have an even color, and melt in the mouth.

WHERE TO LEARN MORE

Battistotti, Bruno. *Cheese, A Guide to the World of Cheese and Cheese Making.* Facts on File, 1984.

O'Neil, L. Peat. "Homemade Cheese," *Country Journal.* March/April 1993, pp. 60-63.

Reader's Digest: How in the World? Reader's Digest, 1990.

Chocolate

History

Cocoa trees originated in South America's river valleys, and, by the seventh century, the Mayan Indians had brought them north into Mexico. In addition to the Mayans, many other Central American Indians, including the Aztecs and the Toltecs, seem to have grown cocoa trees, and the words "chocolate" and "cocoa" both come from the Aztec language.

When Hernando Cortés, Hernando de Soto Pizarro, and other Spanish explorers arrived in Central America in the fifteenth century, they noted that cocoa beans were considered precious enough to be used as money. They also recorded that the upper class natives drank cacahuatl, a frothy, stimulating beverage made from roasted cocoa beans blended with red pepper, vanilla, and water.

At first the Spanish found the bitter flavor of unsweetened cacahuatl undrinkable, but they gradually changed the recipe to create a drink more appealing to the European tastes. Grinding sugar, cinnamon, cloves, anise, almonds, hazelnuts, vanilla, orange-flower water, and musk with dried cocoa beans, they heated the mixture to create a paste (as with many popular recipes today, variations were common). They then smoothed this paste on the broad, flat leaves of the plantain tree, (a tropical plant which produces a banana-like fruit), let it harden, and removed the resulting slabs of chocolate.

To make chocalatl, the direct ancestor of our hot chocolate, they dissolved these slabs, or tablets, in hot water and a thin corn broth (water in which corn has been boiled). They then stirred the liquid until it was bub-

With an annual consumption rate of around 14 pounds (6 kilograms) per person, chocolate is as popular as a non-essential food can be.

Chocolate in a variety of forms.

bly, perhaps to distribute the fats from the chocolate paste evenly (cocoa beans contain more than fifty percent cocoa butter by weight).

When missionaries and explorers returned to Spain with hot chocolate, they encountered resistance from the powerful Catholic Church, which argued that the beverage, contaminated by its pagan origins, was bound to corrupt Christians who drank it. But the praise of returning conquistadors—Cortés himself designated chocalatl as "the divine drink that builds up resistance and fights fatigue"—overshadowed the church's dire predictions.

Chocolate cravings soon spread to England, where the drink was

During the 1700s, the famous Swedish botanist Carolus Linnaeus gave the treat a formal, scientific name: Theobroma cacao, "the food of the gods."

Desserts use chocolate for both taste and presentation.

served in "chocolate houses"—upscale, fancy versions of the coffee houses that had sprung up in London during the 1600s. In the mid-seventeenth century, milk chocolate was invented by an Englishman, Sir Hans Sloane. Sloane had lived in Jamaica for several years and observed how the people there seemed to thrive on both cocoa products and milk. He then began to dissolve chocolate tablets in milk rather than water.

Although several naturalists and physicians who traveled extensively in the Americas noted that the people there ate solid chocolate lozenges (four-sided tablet or drop), many Europeans believed that eating chocolate in this form would cause indigestion. As this fear proved unfounded, cookbooks began to include recipes for chocolate candy.

Coarse and crumbly textural problems were solved in 1828, when Dutch chocolate maker Conrad van Houten invented a screw press that could squeeze most of the butter out of cocoa beans. Van Houten's press refined chocolate by permitting the separation of cocoa beans into cocoa powder and cocoa butter. Dissolved in hot liquid, the powder created a beverage far tastier than previous chocolate drinks. Blended with regular ground cocoa beans, the cocoa butter made chocolate paste smoother and easier to blend with sugar.

In 1876 a Swiss candy maker named Daniel Peter further refined chocolate production, using the dried milk recently invented by the Nestle company to make solid milk chocolate. In 1913 Jules Sechaud, another Swiss candy-lover, developed a technique for making chocolate shells filled with other confections (sweetened foods). Well before World War I (1914-1918), chocolate had become one of the most popular taste treats, though it was still quite expensive.

Chocolate Today

Hershey Foods, one of a number of American chocolate-making companies founded during the nineteenth and early twentieth centuries, made chocolate more affordable and available. Today the most famous—though not the largest—chocolate producer in the United States, the company was founded by Milton Hershey, who invested the fortune he'd earned making caramels in a Pennsylvania chocolate factory.

When he turned to chocolate making, Hershey decided to use the same fresh milk that had made his caramels so flavorful. He also decided to use mass production techniques that would enable him to sell large quantities of chocolate, individually wrapped and affordably priced. For decades after Hershey began manufacturing them in 1904, Hershey bars cost only a nickel. The candy was so popular that the company didn't even advertise them until 1968.

Another company, M&M/Mars, has branched out to produce dozens of non-chocolate products, yet since its founding in 1922, M&M/Mars has produced many of the country's most enduringly popular chocolate confections. The company's success began with the Milky Way bar, which was cheaper to produce than pure chocolate because its malt flavor derived from nougat, a mixture of egg whites and corn syrup. The Snickers and Three Musketeers bars, which also featured cost-cutting nougat centers, soon followed.

A variety of popular chocolate candy.

During the 1930s soldiers fighting in the Spanish Civil War dreamed up the idea for M&Ms. To prevent the chocolate candy from melting in their pockets, these soldiers had protected it with a sugary coating. The Mars company borrowed the idea to create its most popular, colorful, pill-sized product. "Melts in your mouth—not in your hand," was M&M's popular advertising slogan.

Chocolate Ingredients

Though other ingredients are added, most notably sugar or other sweeteners, flavorings, and sometimes potassium carbonate (used to make so-called dutch cocoa—a darker, more mild chocolate), cocoa beans are the primary component of chocolate.

Cocoa trees are evergreens that grow best within 20 degrees of the equator, at altitudes of between 100 (30.48 centimeters) and 1,000 (304.8 centimeters) feet above sea level. Native to South and Central America, the trees are currently grown on commercial plantations in such places as

- *Cocoa butter melts at about 97 degrees Fahrenheit, slightly below body temperature—a property which enhances the melt-in-your-mouth pleasure of chocolate.*

- *White chocolate contains no cocoa solids, so is not technically chocolate, but a small amount of cocoa butter lends it a chocolate fragrance.*

- *Chocolate does not cause acne.*

- *A chocolate bar contains about six milligrams of caffeine, compared to 115 milligrams in a cup of coffee.*

Malaysia, Brazil, Ecuador, and West Africa. West Africa currently produces nearly three quarters of the world's 75,000 ton annual cocoa bean crop, while Brazil is the largest producer in the Western Hemisphere.

Because they are relatively delicate, the trees can be harmed by full sun, fungi, and insects. To minimize such damage, they are usually planted with the hardier rubber or banana trees. These crops afford protection from the sun and provide plantation owners with an alternative income if the cocoa trees fail.

The fruit of the cocoa tree are pods 6 to 10 inches (15.24-25.4 centimeters) long and 3 to 4 inches (7.62-10.16 centimeters) in diameter. Most trees bear only about 30 to 40 pods, each of which contains between 20 and 40 inch-long (2.54 centimeters) beans in a gummy liquid. The pods ripen in three to four months, and, because of the even, warm climate in which the trees grow, they ripen continuously throughout the year. However, the greatest number of pods are harvested between May and December.

Of the 30 to 40 pods on a typical cocoa tree, no more than half will be ripe at any given time. Only the ripe fruits can be harvested, as only they will produce top quality ingredients. The pods are cut from the trees with machetes (large, heavy knives with broad blades) or knives mounted on poles (the trees are too delicate to be climbed). Mature pods are opened on the plantation with a large knife or machete so the beans inside can be removed by hand.

Still entwined with pulp (the soft, moist insides) from the pods, the seeds are piled on the ground, where they heat beneath the sun for several days (some plantations also dry the beans mechanically, if necessary). Enzymes (proteins) from the pulp combine with wild, airborne yeasts (fungi) to cause a small amount of fermentation (foam or froth) that will make the final product even more appetizing. During the fermenting process, the beans reach a temperature of about 125 degrees Fahrenheit. This prevents the beans from sprouting while being shipped to a factory, and helps break down the beans' cell walls. Once the beans have sufficiently fermented, they will be stripped of the remaining pulp and dried.

Next, they are graded for size and quality and bagged in sacks weighing from 130 to 200 pounds (59.02-90.8 kilograms). They are then stored until they are inspected, after which they are shipped to an auction and sold to chocolate makers.

The Manufacturing Process

Roasting, hulling, and crushing the beans

1 Once a company has received a shipment of cocoa beans at its processing plant, the beans are roasted, first on screens and then in revolving cylinders through which heated air is blown. Over a period of 30 minutes to 2 hours, the moisture in the beans is reduced from about 7 percent to 1 percent. The roasting process triggers a browning reaction, in which more than 300 different chemicals naturally present in the cocoa beans interact. The beans now begin to develop the rich flavor we associate with chocolate.

2 Roasting also causes the shells to open and break away from the nibs (the meat of the bean). This separation process can be completed by blowing air across the beans as they go through a giant winnowing machine called a cracker and fanner, which loosens the hulls from the beans without crushing them (see fig. 18). The hulls, now separated from the nibs, are usually sold as either mulch or fertilizer. They are also sometimes used as a commercial boiler fuel.

3 Next, the roasted nibs undergo broyage, a process of crushing that takes place in a grinder made of revolving granite blocks. The design of the grinder may vary, but most resemble old-fashioned flour mills. The final product of this grinding process is a thick syrup known as chocolate liquor, made up of small particles of the nib suspended in oil.

4 The next step, refining, during which the liquor is further ground between sets of revolving metal drums. Each successive rolling is faster than the preceding one because the liquor is becoming smoother and flows easier. The ultimate goal is to reduce the size of the particles in the liquor to about .001 inch (.00254 centimeters).

Making cocoa powder

5 If the chocolate being produced is to be cocoa powder, from which hot chocolate and baking mixes are made, the chocolate liquor may be dutched, a process so-named because it was invented by the

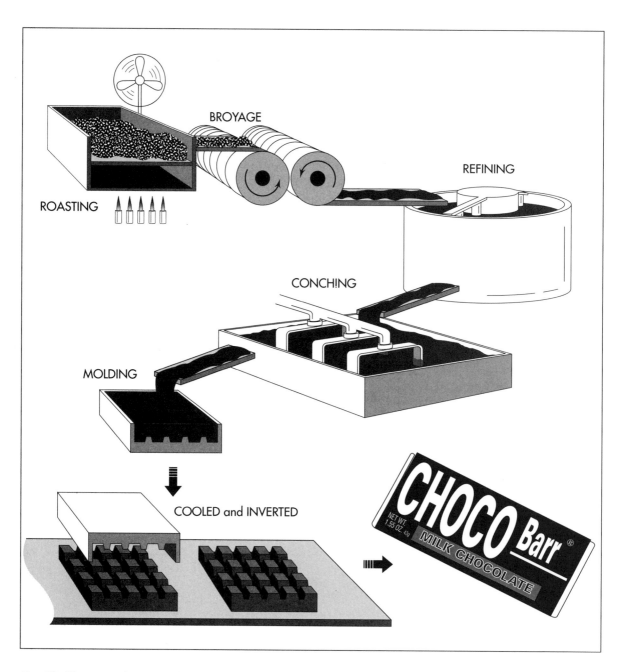

Fig. 18. The cocoa beans are first roasted, causing the bean shells to break away from their center (the nibs). Next, the nibs undergo broyage, a crushing process that takes place in a grinder with revolving granite (rock) blocks. The next step, refining, further grinds the particles and makes the chocolate mass smoother. The mass is then conched, or ground, and agitated in huge open vats. The mass is then poured into molds, cooled, cut, and wrapped.

Dutch chocolate maker Conrad van Houten. In the dutching process, the liquor is treated with an alkaline solution, usually potassium carbonate. This treatment darkens the color of the cocoa, makes its flavor more mild, and reduces the tendency of the nib particles to form clumps in the liquor. The resulting powder is called dutch cocoa.

> *Good News—Chocolate contains small amounts of protein, iron, calcium, niacin, riboflavin, thiamin, potassium, phosphorous and magnesium—all healthy vitamins, minerals, and substances needed in our diets. Bad News—Chocolate is loaded with sugar and fat, practically canceling out any nutritious advantages.*

6 The next step in making cocoa powder is defatting the chocolate liquor, or removing large amounts of butter from it. This is done by further compressing the liquor between rollers, until about half of the fat from its cocoa beans has been released. The resulting solid material, commonly called press cake, is then broken, chopped, or crushed before being sifted to produce cocoa powder. When additives such as sugar or other sweeteners have been blended, this cocoa powder becomes a modern version of chocalatl.

Making chocolate candy

7 If the chocolate being produced is to become candy, the press cake is remixed with some of the removed cocoa butter. The restored cocoa butter is necessary for texture and consistency, and different types of chocolate require different amounts of cocoa butter.

8 The mixture now undergoes a process known as conching, in which it is continuously turned and ground in a huge open vat (see fig. 18). The process's name comes from the shape of older vats, which resembled large conch (sea) shells. The conching process can last from between three hours to three days (more time is not necessarily better, however). This is the most important step in making chocolate. The speed and temperature of the mixing are critical in determining the quality of the final product.

9 Another crucial aspect of conching is the time and rate at which other ingredients are added. The ingredients added during conching determine what type of chocolate is produced: sweet chocolate consists of chocolate liquor, cocoa butter, sugar, and vanilla; milk chocolate contains sweet chocolate with powdered whole milk or whole liquid milk.

Chocolate lovers
judge the quality
of their candy
based on its
glossiness,
sweet smell,
smooth
consistency, and
texture.

10

At the end of the conching process, the chocolate is poured into molds, cooled, cut, and wrapped.

Quality Control

Recipes, exact amounts of ingredients, and even some aspects of processing are carefully guarded secrets, although certain guidelines were set by the 1944 Federal Food, Drug, and Cosmetic Law, as well as more recent laws and regulations. For example, milk chocolate must contain a minimum of 12 percent milk solids and 10 percent chocolate liquor. Sweet chocolate, which contains no milk solids, must contain at least fifteen percent chocolate liquor.

The major companies, however, have a reputation for enforcing strict quality and cleanliness standards. Milton Hershey zealously insisted upon fresh ingredients, and the Mars company boasts that its factory floors harbor fewer bacteria than the average kitchen sink. Moreover, slight imperfections are often enough to prompt the rejection of entire batches of candy.

The Future

Despite its nutritional drawbacks, and regardless of whether or not one accepts the theories about its effects, chocolate seems guaranteed to remain what it has been throughout the twentieth century: food fit for the gods.

WHERE TO LEARN MORE

Morton, Marcia. *Chocolate: An Illustrated History*. Crown Publishers, 1986.
O'Neill, Catherine. *Let's Visit a Chocolate Factory*. Troll Associates, 1988.
The Story of Chocolate. Chocolate Manufacturers' Association of the U.S.A.

Combination Lock

Finding the Right Combination

Combination locks don't open with a key but rather by the careful alignment (lining up) of its interior parts in a definite position. The most common types have a series of three or four interconnected rings or discs inside, that are attached to and turned by a central shaft. Manually rotating the outside knob or dial turns the discs, each of which is "programmed" to stop at a notched opening or gate. However, a four-disc lock must have its dial spun around first to get the lock to move the correct disc.

The knob must first be turned to the right and spun past the first number four times before being allowed to stop beneath the marker. Next, rotating in the opposite direction, the knob must pass the second number three times. Reversing directions again, the user must spin the dial past the third number twice, and so on. When the openings on all the interior rings line up together, they allow projections on a spring-loaded bolt to slide through. This releases the bolt and opens the lock.

Since most locks can use any of 100 million possible combinations, identifying the correct one by chance is highly unlikely.

Combination locks come in two varieties: hand and key change. One kind of hand combination lock that does not use internal wheels is the pushbutton lock, commonly installed in office doors because it offers more security. Pushing three or four buttons in order or together releases

A student opening the combination lock attached to her locker.

a shaft or deadbolt, allowing the door to open. The internal mechanisms operate similarly to those in a padlock.

Padlocks are the simple, portable, detachable locks found on many school lockers and bike locks. Picking these and other low-priced combination locks used to be a game that many students successfully played. With practice, an aspiring lockpick could actually hear the clicks made when the projections on the bolt aligned with the notches on the discs. However, manufacturers of better locks design false gates in the discs to make cracking the lock extremely difficult. Only experts can tell the difference between the three or more false gates and the true gate.

History

The combination lock was invented in China, although historical records provide little specific information about its development. Combination locks came into popular use in the United States in the mid-1800s to secure bank vaults (rooms or compartments for safekeeping money and valuables). The locks, built directly into the vault doors, presented quite a challenge to burglars. Western films were famous for their colorful bank-robbery scenes in which the bad guys tried to break into vaults and make off with the loot.

In 1873 James Sargent foiled many real bank robbers by perfecting a time lock. Coupled with a combination lock, this clever invention kept everyone out of the vault until the clock or clocks that controlled the lock reached the time at which it was set to open, usually once a day.

Lock Materials

A typical combination padlock has twenty component parts (see fig.

20). They are usually made of stainless steel (steel mixed with another metallic element which resists rust) or cold-rolled steel that is plated (covered or coated with a thin layer of some material) to resist rust and corrosion.

In addition to steel, two other materials are essential to the combination lock. Nylon (a strong, resilient, man-made material) is used for the spacers that separate the discs, enabling them to turn independently. Zamak, a zinc alloy (metallic mixture), is molded under pressure to form the bar, shaft, and outside dial.

Combination locks are constructed to last a lifetime, and their parts are not intended to require repair or replacement.

Design

A combination lock's parts can be divided into two categories: internal (inside) and external (outside) components (see fig. 20). Except for the springs when extended, none of the internal parts are longer than two inches (5.08 centimeters) in length.

The internal works of the locking mechanism consist of a lever and its supporting lever post plus a central disc shaft (connected to the center knob which is turned from the outside) around which disc spacers and the combination disc turn. Two, three, or four combination discs are the key precision elements of the lock mechanism, but it is the combination cam, a notched disc, that holds the winning code which will unlock the mechanism. The cam is also attached to the outside combination dial that is turned by the lock's user. The internal disc spring holds the combination discs under tension, enabling the combination to be dialed.

Other internal parts in the lock case include a shackle collar that holds the shackle (the U-shaped piece that detaches from the case when the lock has been opened) in the locked position with a latch. This locking latch fits into a notch in the shackle and either hooks it closed, or releases it to open. Finally an inner case encloses all internal parts and gives the lock extra strength.

External parts include the lock's outer case, the shackle, a back cover, and the combination dial.

The Manufacturing Process

The twenty component parts of the typical combination lock are formed, drawn (hammered, stretched, or stamped into shape), cut, pressed, and molded on a variety of machines, both manual and automatic.

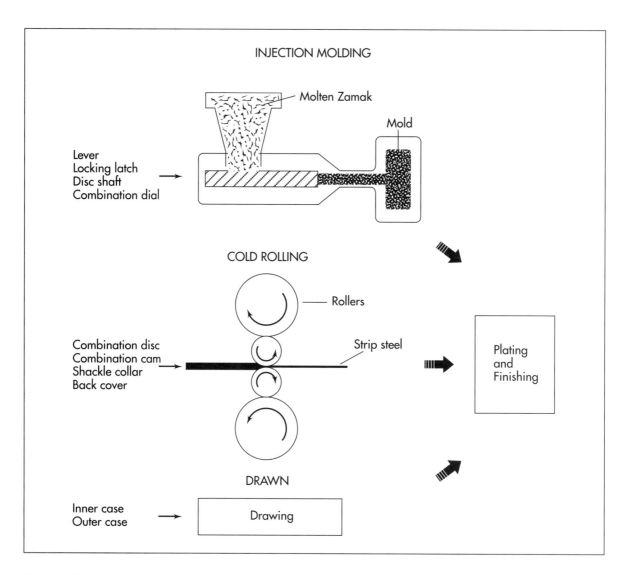

Fig. 19. The various components (elements) in a combination lock are made in a variety of ways. Some components, such as those made from zamak, are injection molded. Other components, such as the combination cam and disc, are cold rolled. Still other components are drawn or molded by machine into the proper shape. Most of the components are then plated (coated) to protect against corrosion.

Making the internal components

1 The lever, locking latch, and disc shaft are all made by injection molding, a process in which molten zamak is poured into a mold and subjected to heat and pressure until it solidifies into the shape of the mold (see fig. 19).

Although the lever post is shaped at room temperature, it is also formed under high pressure. The combination disc and the cam are made of cold-rolled—passed under huge rolls without being heated—flat strip steel (see fig. 19). Then the steel is put in a blanking die, a sophisticated cookie cutter, which cuts (or blanks) out the properly shaped piece.

The internal disc spring is made from stainless steel round wire and produced on a spring winder that automatically twists and turns the wire to form the traditional coil spring.

The shackle collar, like the combination disc and cam, is made from cold-rolled flat strip steel that is cut (blanked) in a blanking die. The inner case is produced from flat steel strip and drawn into a cup-like shape (see fig. 19). This process requires great pressure to stretch and compress the steel as it is pressed or drawn around a die, whose shape it takes.

Making the outer parts

2 The outer case is manufactured similarly to the inner case but from stainless steel sheet instead of strip. The back cover, also stainless steel, is cut from a blanking die.

The durable shackle is made of round bar stock on a screw machine, then formed to its U-shape and notched to accept the locking latch. It is finally annealed (heated by extremely high temperature before being cooled in water) to make it resistant to hacksaws and bolt cutters.

The combination dial, also zamak, is injection molded, then chromized. This process involves heating the dial in a salt bath rich in chromium (a shiny metal which resists tarnish and rust). The steel absorbs the chromium, which hardens on the surface as it rapidly cools. Then the dial is painted black, and white wiped—which leaves the numbers highlighted against the black face.

Plating the components

3 Several plating and finishing processes can be used to protect the components against corrosion. The lever, disc shaft, combination cam, and dial are chromized. The inner case, shackle collar, and lever post are all cadmium-plated (cadmium is a bluish-white metallic element used in rust-proofing). The shackle and locking latch are copper nickel-plated. The outer case, of stainless steel, is mechanically polished to a shine.

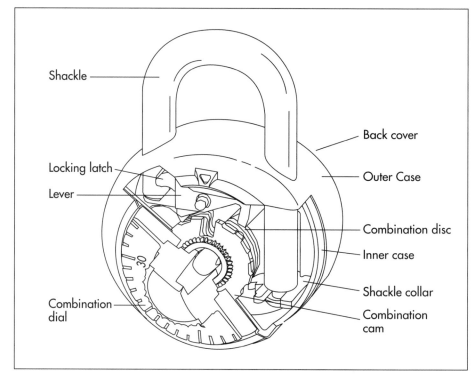

Shackle

Back cover

Outer Case

Locking latch

Lever

Combination disc

Inner case

Shackle collar

Combination dial

Combination cam

Fig. 20. A fully constructed combination lock.

Assembling the lock

4 Lock components are assembled with careful precision. The back plate disc shaft, combination cam, and spacers form one sub-assembly. The outer and inner cases are riveted (bolted) together and then pierced at the point where the shackle is inserted. The combination dial, outer and inner case unit, and combination cam are then fastened together. Finally, these sub-assemblies and the remaining parts are fitted together. The lock case is closed and the edges folded over and sealed. Conventional hardware fasteners that can be released with the proper tool are not used.

Labeling and packaging

5 The last step is the application of a removable tag or label to the lock. On this tag is the all-important combination, which is chosen randomly by machine. A typical combination lock is sold in blister

pack, a rigid molded plastic with cardboard backing, although locks may also be individually boxed.

Quality Control

Before any lock is packaged, many manufacturers completely test the locking and unlocking sequence. Other inspections and measurements are performed by individual operators at their stations during both manufacturing and assembly. Combination locks today enjoy a reputation for excellent reliability and durability.

Future Locks

Burglars beware! Manufacturers are working on production of foolproof computer-controlled combination locks. The computerized locks will only open after the correct code is entered. Its design allows for over 1 million possible combinations. One drawback—the locks are costly—around $600. Still, for bankers and others willing to pay the price, safecracking may soon be a worry of the past.

A safe with a combination lock.

WHERE TO LEARN MORE

All About Locks and Locksmithing. Hawthorne Books, 1972.
Combination Lock Principles. Gordon Press Publishers, 1986.
The Complete Book of Locks and Locksmithing. Tab Books, 1991.
Tchudi, Stephen. *Lock and Key*. Charles Scribner's Sons, 1993.

Compact Disc

A standard CD can store up to 74 minutes of rock, rap, or rhythm and blues. However, most CDs contain only about 50 minutes of music.

Sound and Science

Ever since the invention of the phonograph in 1876, music has been a popular source of home entertainment. In recent years, the compact disc has captured the attention and dollars of the mass music market.

A compact disc, or CD, is an optical (uses light sensitive equipment) storage medium with digital data (information translated into a numeric code) recorded on it. The digital data can be in the form of audio (sound), video (visual), or computer information. When the CD is played, the information is read or detected by a tightly focused light source called a laser. This explanation will focus on audio compact discs, which are used to play back recorded music.

History

The history of the compact disc can be traced back to the development of digital electronic technology in the 1960s. Although the first applications of this new science were not in the recording area, researchers soon found it to be especially well-suited for the music industry.

During the same period, many companies started experimenting with optical information storage and laser technology. Among these companies, electronic giants Sony and Philips made the most notable progress in this area.

By the 1970s, digital and optical technologies (the application of science to numbers and light) had reached a level where they could be combined to develop a single audio system. These technologies provided

A compact disc.

solutions to the three main challenges faced by the developers of digital audio.

Challenges and Solutions

The first challenge was to find a suitable method for recording audio signals in digital format, a process known as audio encoding (translating sounds into a numeric code). A practical method of audio encoding was developed from the theories published by C. Shannon in 1948. This method, known as pulse code modulation (PCM), is a technique that sam-

One of the first Sony compact disc players available to consumers.

ples or listens to a sound during a short time interval and converts the sample to a numerical value that is then stored for later use.

The storing of audio signals in digital form requires a large amount of data. For instance, to store one second of music requires one million bits of data. The next challenge, therefore, was to find a suitable storage medium—something small enough to be practical but able to hold all the codes necessary for recording a song, album, or symphony. The solution to this problem came in the form of optical discs. An optical disc can store large amounts of data tightly pressed together. For example, 1 million bits of data on a CD can occupy an area smaller than a pinhead. This information is read with a sophisticated laser beam that is capable of focusing on an area as small as 1/2500th of an inch.

The final challenge of a digital sound system was to process all that closely-packed information on compact discs quickly enough to produce continuous music. The solution was provided by the development of integrated circuit technology, which allows the processing of millions of bits of data in just microseconds.

By the late 1970s, a common set of standards for the optical storage discs had been developed by the joint efforts of Sony and Philips. A partnership of 35 hardware manufacturers agreed to adopt this standard in 1981 and the first compact discs and compact disc players were introduced to music-lovers in 1982.

The agreement forged between Sony and Philips to share their compact disc ideas greatly simplified life for both musicians and their fans. The two companies are strong competitors and could have developed CDs and players which were not compatible. Consumers would have been limited to playing only those CDs which worked on one type of player. Cooperation between the companies paid off for everyone: CD sales now top both records and tapes, and profits are shared by all.

LIFE AFTER DEATH

The tendency of records and tapes to deteriorate over time seemed to silence the songs of older artists. Fortunately for fans, a method of transferring aging classics from imperfect sources onto superior CDs works very well. Called "digital remastering," the sound editing and digital recoding techniques are capable of erasing the static and even filling in missing notes from old, damaged recordings.

CD Materials

Compact discs look small and simple but the technology required to make them is complex. CDs consist of three layers of materials: A base layer made of a strong plastic, a thin layer of aluminum coating over the plastic, and a clear protective acrylic. Some manufacturers use a silver or gold layer instead of the aluminum layer in their compact discs.

Design

The compact disc is designed according to strict standards established by Sony and Philips, and all can be played on the same type of CD players. A CD is 4.72 inches (120 millimeters) in diameter and .047 inches (1.2 millimeters) thick. The positioning hole in the middle is .59 of an inch (15 millimeters) in diameter. A CD usually weighs around .53 of an ounce (15 grams).

A standard CD can store up to 74 minutes of data. However, most CDs contain only about 50 minutes of music, all of which is recorded on only one side of the CD (the underside). Data is recorded on the CD in a continuous spiral starting from the inside and moving outward.

This spiral track consists of a series of indentations called pits, separated by flat sections called lands (see fig. 22). A tiny laser beam moving along the track reflects light back to a photo sensor (a device that changes a light code into electric signals). The sensor sees more light when it is on a land than when it is on a pit, and these variations in light intensity (on-and-off flashes) are translated into electrical signals that represent the music originally recorded.

The Manufacturing Process

Compact discs must be manufactured under very clean and dust free conditions in a "clean room," which is kept free from nearly all dust particles. The air in the room is specially filtered to keep out dirt, and workers in the room must wear special clothing.

Preparing the disc master

1 The original music is first recorded onto a digital audio tape. Next, the resulting audio program is transferred to a $\frac{3}{4}$-inch (1.9 centimeters) video tape, and then data (called subcodes) used for indexing and tracking (organizing and finding) the music is added to the audio data on the tape. At this point, the tape is called a pre-master.

2 The pre-master tape is used to create the disc master (also called the glass master), which is a disc made from specially prepared glass (see fig. 21). The glass is polished to a smooth finish and coated with a layer of adhesive (glue) and a layer of photoresist material. The disc is approximately 9.45 inches (240 millimeters) in diameter and .24 of an inch (six millimeters) thick. After the adhesive and photoresist are applied, the disc is cured (finished or preserved) in an oven.

3 Next, both the pre-master tape and the disc master are put into a complex laser cutting machine. The machine plays back the audio program on the pre-master tape. As it does so, the program is transferred to a device called a CD encoder, which in turn generates an electrical signal. This signal powers a laser beam, which "cuts" grooves into the photoresist coating on the glass disc (the disc master).

4 The grooves that have been exposed are then etched (cut) away by chemicals; these etched grooves will form the pits of the CD's surface. A metal coating, usually silver, is then applied to the disc. The disc master now contains the exact pit-and-land track that the finished CD will have.

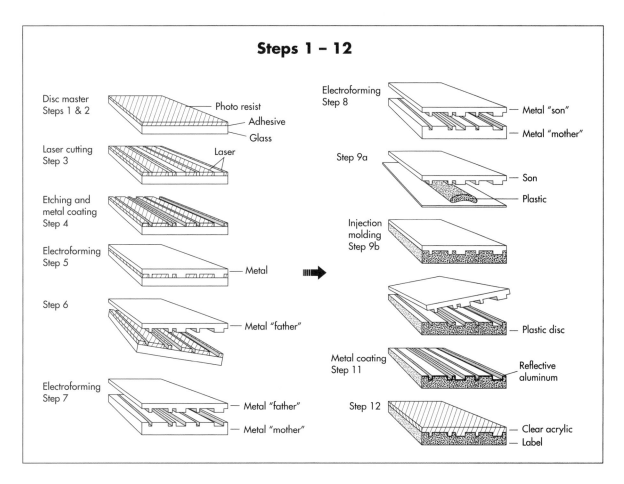

Steps 1 – 12

Disc master
Steps 1 & 2
— Photo resist
— Adhesive
— Glass

Laser cutting
Step 3
Laser

Etching and
metal coating
Step 4

Electroforming
Step 5
— Metal

Step 6
— Metal "father"

Electroforming
Step 7
— Metal "father"
— Metal "mother"

Electroforming
Step 8
— Metal "son"
— Metal "mother"

Step 9a
— Son
— Plastic

Injection
molding
Step 9b

— Plastic disc

Metal coating
Step 11
— Reflective
aluminum

Step 12
— Clear acrylic
— Label

Fig. 21. Making a compact disc involves first preparing a glass "disc master." This master is then encoded with the desired information and put through a series of electroforming steps. In electroforming, metal layers are deposited on the glass master using electric currents. When the final master version is ready, its information is transferred onto a plastic disc. A reflective aluminum layer is applied, followed by a clear acrylic protective layer, and finally the label.

Electroforming

5 After etching, the disc master undergoes a process called electro-forming, in which another metal layer such as nickel is deposited onto the disc's surface. The term "electro" is used because the metal is applied using an electric current. The disc is bathed in a metallic solution, and as the electric current is applied, a layer of metal forms on the disc master. The thickness of this metal layer is strictly controlled.

6 Next, the newly applied metal layer is pulled apart from the disc master, which is put aside. The metal layer, or "father", contains a negative impression of the disc master track; in other words, the track on the metal layer is an exact copy, but in reverse, of the track on the disc master.

7 The metal father then undergoes further electroforming to produce one or more "mothers," which are simply metal layers that again have positive impressions of the original disc master track. Using the same electroforming process, each mother then produces a "son" (also called a stamper) with a negative impression of the track. It is the son that is used to create the actual CD.

8 After being separated from the mother, the metal son is then rinsed, dried, polished and put in a punching machine that cuts out the center hole and forms the desired outside diameter.

Making copies

9 The metal son is then put into a hollow mold—a die—of the proper disc shape in an injection molding machine. Molten plastic is then poured into this die to form around the metal son. When cool, the plastic is shaped in a positive impression of the original disc master track— with the pits and grooves formed into one side.

10 The center hole is then punched out of plastic disc, which is transparent at this stage. Next, the disc is scanned for flaws such as water bubbles, dust particles, and warps (curves or bends). If a flaw is found, the disc must be discarded.

11 If the disc meets the quality standards, it is then coated with an extremely thin, reflective layer of aluminum. The coating is applied using vacuum deposition. In this process, aluminum is put into a vacuum chamber (a completely empty room or compartment) and heated to the point of evaporation, which allows it to be applied evenly to the plastic disc.

12 Finally, a clear acrylic plastic is applied to the disc to help protect the underlying layers from physical damage such as scratches. After the label is applied, the compact disc is complete and ready for packaging and shipment.

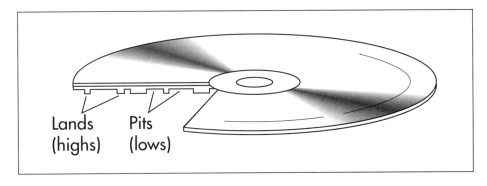

Fig. 22. A finished compact disc contains a series of tracks or indentations called "lands" and "pits." A CD player uses a laser beam to read this up-and-down code and convert the reflection first into an electrical signal and then into music.

Quality Control

A compact disc is a very precise and accurate product. The microscopic size of the data does not allow for any errors in the manufacturing process. The smallest of dust particles can cause a disc to be unreadable.

The first quality control concern is to ensure that the "clean room" environment is properly monitored, with controlled temperature, humidity, and filtering systems. Beyond that, quality control checkpoints are built into the manufacturing process. The disc master, for instance, is inspected for smoothness and its photoresist surface for proper thickness by means of laser equipment. At later stages in the process, such as before and after the aluminum and acrylic coatings are applied, the disc is checked automatically for warps, bubbles, dust particles, and encoding errors on the spiral track. This mechanical checking is combined with human inspection using polarized light, which allows the human eye to spot defective pits in the track.

In addition to checking the discs, the equipment used to manufacture them must be carefully maintained. The laser cutting machine, for instance, must be very stable, because any vibration would make proper cutting impossible. If strict quality control is not maintained, the rejection rate of CDs can be very high.

Future Tune Technology

The massive storage capabilities, accuracy of data, and durability of materials will continue to make compact discs a popular medium for music and video. The hottest new product stirring public interest is CD-Interactive or CD-I, a multimedia system that allows users to interact with computers and television.

Manufacturers continue to streamline and improve compact disc production. They already require smaller facilities and less human involvement in the process, resulting in lower CD rejection rates. In the first decade of the CD industry, the manufacturing and quality control processes have become almost completely automated, or performed by machines.

WHERE TO LEARN MORE

Library of Science Technology. Marshall Cavendish Corporation, 1989.
Macaulay, David. *The Way Things Work.* Houghton Mifflin Company, 1988.
Pohlmann, Ken C. *The Compact Disk Handbook,* 2nd ed., A-R Editions, 1992.
Reader's Digest: How in the World?, Reader's Digest, 1990.

Eyeglass Lens

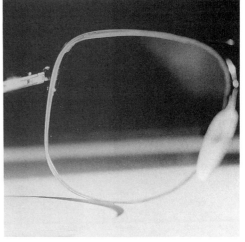

Vision Quest

More than 80 million Americans correct their vision with optical lenses. People put their world into proper focus with fashionable eyeglasses or almost-invisible contact lenses. Both are available in styles to suit every taste, plain or fancy, clear or tinted.

History

Eyeglass lenses are glass or plastic optical (sight, vision) items that fit inside eyewear frames and enhance and/or correct the wearer's vision. The magnifying glass, invented in the early 1200s, was the first optical lens used for enhancing vision. These lenses were made from a transparent quartz (hard, clear crystal or mineral) and beryl (transparent blue-green mineral—aquamarine). The invention led to the critical discovery that when reflective surfaces were ground to certain angles they could correct faulty vision.

In the late thirteenth century, Alessando di Spina, an Italian monk, introduced eyewear to the general public. As demand for eyewear increased, heavy and expensive quartz and beryl lenses were replaced by glass lenses. Through the ages people suffered to see clearly by enduring heavy inventions which pinched the nose, pulled on the ears, and tied around the head before the eighteenth century invention of comfortable eyeglass sidearms.

The convex lens (thicker in the middle, thinner at the edges) was the first optical lens used in glasses made to correct farsightedness (the ability to see

More than 80 percent of all eyeglasses worn today have lightweight plastic lenses.

In 1784 Benjamin Franklin invented bifocals by dividing a lens into distant and near vision sections for people who needed both.

objects better from a distance). Other corrective lenses followed, including the concave lens (thinner in the middle with thicker edges) for the correction of nearsightedness (the inability to see distant objects clearly).

Plastic as well as glass lenses are produced by successive stages of fine grinding, polishing, and shaping. While the same process is used to produce lenses for telescopes, microscopes, binoculars, cameras, and various projectors, such lenses are usually larger and thicker and require greater precision and power. This article will focus on plastic eyeglass lenses.

In the past, opticians (people who make lenses and eyeglasses) relied on separate optical laboratories (places equipped for specialized scientific research) to produce eyeglass lenses. Today, there are a number of full-service optical outlets (offices or stores) that produce lenses on-site, often while the customer waits.

However, optical outlets do receive lens "blanks"—plastic pieces already formed to close-to-exact size with different curves ground into the front of the lens—from optical laboratories. Blanks with different curves are used for specific optical prescriptions (doctors' or opticians' orders).

Protective goggles and eye guards for athletes, which are becoming the standard on many fields and courts, also can be purchased at an optical outlet. The safest models have strong polycarbonate plastic lenses, no detachable parts, and if they're worn outdoors, a coating that will filter out harmful ultraviolet sunlight.

Lens Materials

The plastic blanks received from optical laboratories are round pieces

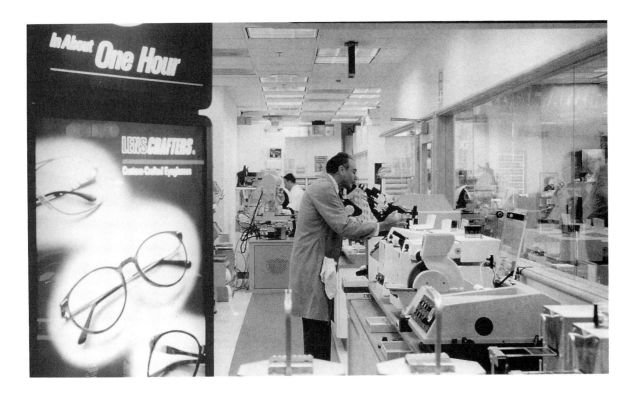

An optical lab/store.

of plastic such as polycarbonate (a strong plastic similar to the material used in airplane windshields) approximately .75 inch (1.9 centimeters) thick and similar in size to eyeglass frames, though slightly larger. Most finished eyeglass lenses are ground to at least .25 inch (.63 centimeter), but this thickness may vary depending upon the particular optical prescription or "power" required. Other materials used to produce eyeglass lenses are:

- Adhesive tape
- A liquid with a lead alloy (metallic mixture) base
- Metal
- Dyes and tints

High-Style Eye Designs

Eyeglass lenses are designed in a variety of shapes to match eyeglass frames. The thickness and shape of each lens varies depending on the

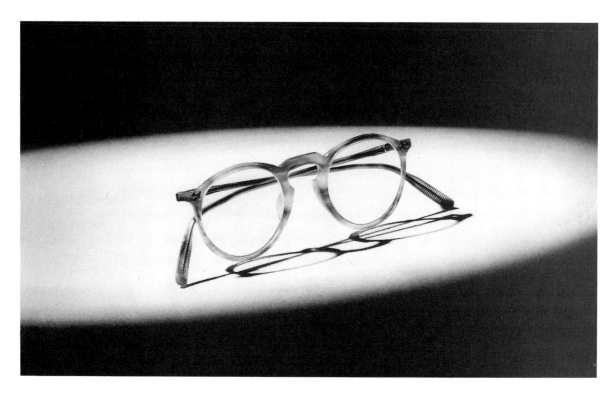

A pair of eyeglasses.

amount and type of correction required. In addition, the bevel (angle) surrounding the edge of a lens is designed to hold the lens in the desired eyeglass frames. Some lenses, such as those for metal and rimless frames, require more detailed edging to fit securely in the frames.

Convex and concave lenses, known as spherical lenses, require one ground curve per lens, while more curves are required to correct astigmatism (the inability to see sharp or distinct images). The degree and angle of the curve or curves in a lens determine its optical strength.

Various lens treatments and tints are added after the lenses are shaped but before they are inserted in frames. The coatings are added by dipping the lenses into heated metal bins filled with the treatment or tint. The treatments and tints available include:

- various tints and colors for sunglasses,
- ultraviolet light tints,
- durability and impact-resistant treatments, and
- scratch-resistant treatments.

Among the latest advances in tints is the light-sensitive tint, which combines the advantages of regular clear lenses with the protection of sunglasses. These lenses adjust to the amount of sunlight being radiated (turning darker in daylight and lighter in the dark), thus providing sun protection only when needed.

Various grades of plastic are used for eyewear, but the most popular is the "Featherweight," an impact-resistant polycarbonate plastic (similar to the material used in airplane windshields). This type of plastic lens is more durable and 30 percent thinner and lighter than regular plastic lenses. It is also the more expensive lens. Other types include the standard "CR 39" trade name plastic lens, and the "High Index" plastic lens, which is 20 percent thinner and lighter than ordinary plastic lenses.

EXPRESS YOURSELF

Frame materials (such as metal, wood, or plastic), temple decorations (including rhinestones, sparkles, and cartoon characters), and color (both lens and frame) give the wearer a lot to think about while selecting the next pair of eyeglasses.

Throughout the years, eyeglass frames have sported a wide variety of shapes and sizes from wide-eyed rounds, to studious squares, to pointy cat's eyes.

The Manufacturing Process

The following procedure assumes the lenses are being made at an optical laboratory.

1 The optical laboratory technician enters the optical prescription for a pair of plastic lenses in the laboratory's computer. The computer then provides a printout specifying the additional information needed for producing the required prescription.

2 Based on this information, the technician selects the appropriate plastic lens blanks. Each blank is placed in a prescription tray along with the customer's eyeglass frames and the original work order (see fig. 23). The prescription tray will remain with the technician throughout the production process.

Different curves are pre-ground into the front of the plastic blanks and the technician must select the blank that matches the optical prescription required for each lens. The rest of the optical prescription, or power, must be ground into the back of the lens.

Blocking

3 The technician places the lenses in a lensometer, an instrument used to locate and mark the "optical center"—the point that should be centered over the customer's pupil—of the lens blanks (see fig. 23).

Next, adhesive tape is attached to the front of each blank to keep the front from being scratched during the "blocking" process. The technician then places one lens blank at a time in a "blocker" machine, which contains a heated lead alloy that fuses the block to the front of the blank. The blocks are used to hold each lens in place during the grinding and polishing processes.

4 Next, the technician places each blank into a generator— a grinding machine that is set for the optical prescription (see fig. 24). The generator grinds the appropriate optical curves into the back of each lens. After this step, the lenses must be "fined," or polished.

Polishing

5 The technician selects a metal lens lap—a mold matching the optical prescription of the lens, and both lenses are placed in the fining machine with the back of each in the appropriate lap. The front of each lens is then polished in a series of fining operations. First, each lens is rubbed against an abrasive fining pad made of soft sandpaper. After a second fining pad made of a smooth plastic is placed over the original sandpaper pad, the lens is polished again, as the fining machine rotates the pads in a circular motion while water flows over the lenses. After the initial fining process is completed, the two pads are peeled off and thrown away.

6 Next, the laps are removed from each lens and soaked in hot water for a few moments. The laps are then reattached to the lenses and placed in the fining machine, where the third and final fining pad is attached. The fining machine rotates the pads in a circular motion while a polishing mixture flows over the lenses.

7 The lenses are removed from the fining machine, and the block attached to each lens is gently detached with a small hammer. Then, the tape is removed from each lens by hand. The laps are sterilized before they are used to hold other lenses.

8 Each lens is marked "L" or "R" with a red grease pencil, indicating which is the left and right lens. After the lenses are again placed in the lensometer to check and mark the optical center and inspect the other curves necessary for the proper optical prescription, a leap pad—a small, round metal holder— is then attached to the back of each lens.

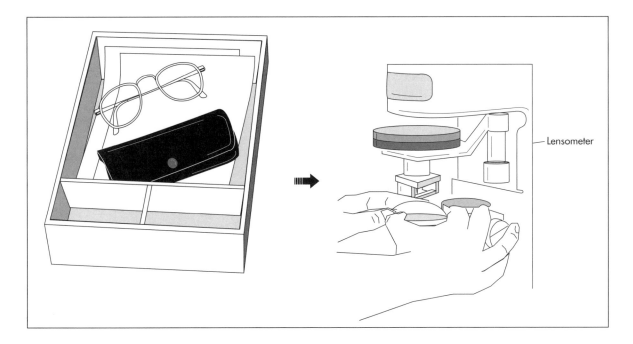

Fig. 23. After the lens blanks are received from the factory, the optical laboratory technician selects the appropriate blanks and puts them in a lensometer. This is an instrument used to locate and mark the "optical center"—the point in the lens that should be centered over the customer's pupil (the center of the eye).

Beveling

9 Next, the technician selects the lens pattern that matches the shape of the eyeglass frames and inserts the pattern and the lenses into an edging machine (see fig. 24). The machine grinds each lens to its proper shape and places a bevel around the edge of the lens so that the lens will fit the eyeglass frames. Water flows over the lens throughout this process.

10 If the lenses require additional grinding, the process is done by hand using a mounted power grinder. This step is necessary for lenses to be inserted in metal or rimless frames, which require more precise bevels.

11 Finally, the lenses are dipped into the desired treatment or tint container. After drying, they are ready to be inserted into the desired frames. The optical laboratory may send the lenses back

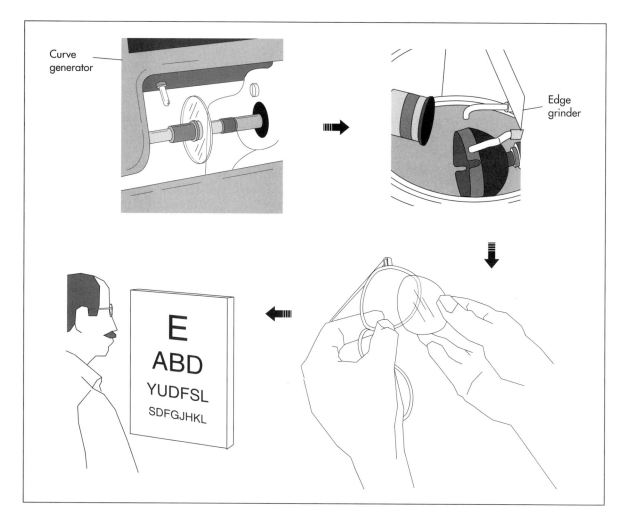

Fig. 24. The technician must still grind curves into the back of the lens. This is done in a curve generator. After polishing the lenses, they are put in an edge grinder, which grinds each lens to its proper shape and places a bevel around the edge so that the lens will fit the eyeglass frames. Following any necessary tint applications, the lenses are put into the frames and tested by the wearer.

to the optical outlet without the frames, in which case the optical outlet will insert them in the frames.

Environmental Concerns

Manufacturers must be aware if any of the materials they use in production are hazardous to the environment. Any materials or chemicals which are left over must be disposed of properly. By-products, or waste from this manufacturing process, include plastic dust or fine shavings and a liquid polishing compound consisting of chemicals. The waste material is placed in metal bins for 48 hours along with sanitation compounds (a mixture that will make the material safe.)

Quality Control

Plastic eyeglass lenses must meet rigid standards set by the American National Standards Institute and the Food and Drug Administration (FDA). In addition, all licensed optical laboratories belong to the National Optical Association, which requires members to follow strict rules regarding quality and safety.

Throughout the normal production process, plastic lenses undergo four basic inspections. Three of these occur in the laboratory and the fourth occurs at the optical outlet before the eyeglasses are given to a customer. Other periodic inspections may also be advised. The four inspections involve checking the optical prescription prior to the production process and verifying the optical center placement; visually checking lenses for scratches, chips, rough edges, or other blemishes; visually checking the optical prescription before the lenses are viewed in the lensometer, and verifying optics while the lenses are in the lensometer; and measuring and verifying frame size and fit with a ruler.

WHERE TO LEARN MORE

Gordon, Lucy L. "Eyeglasses Yesterday and Today," *Wilson Library Bulletin*. March 1992, pp. 40-5.

How Your Eyeglasses Are Made. Optical Laboratories Association.

Macaulay, David. *The Way Things Work*. Houghton Mifflin Company, 1988.

Panati, Charles. *Extraordinary Origins of Everyday Things*. Harper & Row, 1987.

Reader's Digest: How in the World? Reader's Digest, 1990.

Floppy Disk

Although floppy disks can neither store as much data nor retrieve it as quickly as conventional (magnetic) disks, they have become extremely popular in situations where flexibility, low cost, and easy use are important.

Solid Info on Floppies

Despite the goofy name, floppies are serious state-of-the-art, high-tech business. A floppy disk is a portable computer storage device that permits easy handling of data (information). Commonly used with personal computers, notebook computers, and word processors, floppy disks consist of flat, circular plates made of metal or plastic and coated with iron oxide (a magnetic material that can record data). When a disk is inserted into the disk drive of a computer, information can be magnetically imprinted (recorded) on this coating. Later location and retrieval of this data is easily accessible.

History

Magnetic storage can be traced back to the 1900 World's Fair, where a Danish engineer named Valdemar Poulsen displayed a telegraphone. This machine contained steel wire on which Poulsen magnetically recorded a speech. His invention caused much excitement in the scientific community and introduced the use of magnetic storage media. During the next few decades, a wide variety of magnetic recording devices were developed, including the floppy disk.

Magnetic disks, first used to store data in 1962, were used to provide extra memory in high-speed computer systems. They were considered ideal for this type of retrieval because a user could access (find) information no matter where it was located on the disk (unlike, for example, a

cassette on which a listener has to play through all the material in order to reach a desired point).

Floppy disks—smaller, more flexible, portable versions of the earlier magnetic disks—were introduced during the 1970s.

How It Works

The principle of magnetic recording is fairly simple. The magnetic recording (writing) and playback (reading) are accomplished by a computer's disk drive, a job something like that of an audio (sound) record player. Data transferred from the computer to the floppy disk is relayed in the form of a binary code (a code based on only two digits, 0s and 1s) and received in the form of magnetic pulses (on and off). In return, the disk sends magnetic patterns that the computer receives as a binary code. Binary (two-number) code is used because it most effectively translates to the natural two-state (pulse-on, pulse-off) characteristics of electricity and magnetism.

Floppy doesn't mean fragile. If you drop one, it won't break. However, floppies can be damaged if exposed to magnets (data may disappear), heat (causes warping), or fluids.

Eight-, 5¼-, and 3½-inch floppy disks.

To record information on a disk, a magnetic head (a computer part that has a tiny electromagnet) contacts the disk's recording surface and magnetically imprints data onto it. It does this by translating the computer's binary (0s and 1s) code into the disk's magnetic (on and off) pulses. Once a magnetic pattern consisting of many pulses (on) and absences (off) has been recorded, the disk holds the encoded information just like a permanent magnet. Retrieving info from the disk involves the opposite process. The magnetic head senses the magnetic pattern on the disk's recorded surface and converts it back into an electronic binary code. The computer then "reads" this information, using it to perform calculations or translating it into letters and figures for display on the monitor.

Size Options

Floppy disks are currently offered in three sizes: an 8-inch (20.32 centimeters) version, a 5¼-inch (3.34 centimeters) version, and a 3½-inch (8.89 centimeters) micro-version. The storage capacities on 8-inch and 5¼-inch disks range from 250 kilobytes (roughly 250,000 characters) to 1.6 megabytes (roughly 1.6 million characters). A 3½-inch disk holds more, from 500 kilobytes to 2 megabytes.

Each type of floppy disk is further identified according to its recording density (depth). A single-sided disk can store data on one side only, while a double-sided disk can store data on both sides. Double density disks can store twice as much data as single density disks, and high density disks have a special coating that enables them to store even more data.

> *Formatting a disk imprints it with a filing system that consists of tracks and sectors. Tracks are concentric (one within another) circles—like a bull's-eye. Each track is divided into small areas called sectors. Formatting also adds a code called a file allocation table (FAT). FAT is like a map or index that tells which sectors are open, and which are already filled with data, and where specific files of information can be found.*

Floppy Materials

All 8-inch and 5¼-inch disks have three major components—the jacket, the liner, and the recording media (see fig. 26). The jacket is made of a vinyl polymer, polyvinyl chloride (PVC) (the kind of plastic used in varying thickness to make water pipes and window blinds), to protect the delicate media against physical damage that might be caused by handling and storage. Inside the jacket, the liner consists of a special-purpose, non-woven, anti-static fabric that is laminated (joined or glued) to the PVC during manufacture. The liner constantly cleans the disk by removing dust and dirt from the surface of the media. The recording media is a flexible layer of Mylar—a polyester film that is an invention of the E. I. du Pont de Nemours & Company—that is only 0.003 of an inch (0.007 centimeters) thick.

The 3½-inch floppy disk is a more complex device with many different components (see fig. 25). It is enclosed in a hard plastic case that protects it from physical damage. The liner consists of a special-purpose fabric similar to that used for 8-inch and 5¼-inch disks, and the recording media is also a Mylar base, 0.003 of an inch thick. The hub, which accurately centers the disk on the drive shaft, is made of stainless steel and attached to the media with an adhesive (sticky) ring. The button that separates the two sides of the shell so the media can move freely inside is made of high-density plastic. The write protect tab, which prevents data from being mistakenly recorded or erased, is plastic. The wiper tab, also

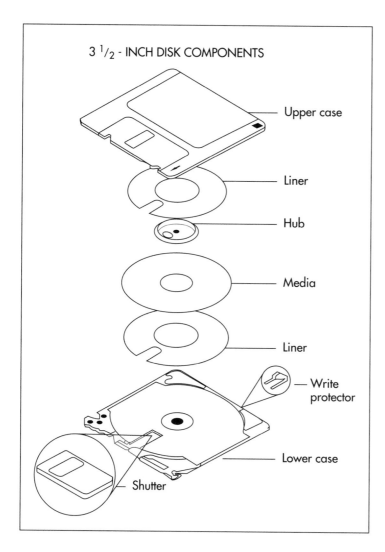

3 ¹/₂ - INCH DISK COMPONENTS

Upper case

Liner

Hub

Media

Liner

Write protector

Lower case

Shutter

Fig. 25. A 3½-inch floppy disk (also called a microfloppy) contains several layers of liner and recording media sandwiched between two hard plastic cases. The hub is a stainless steel piece that accurately centers the disk on the drive shaft. The shutter, also stainless steel, protects the delicate recording media.

plastic, puts pressure on the liner to allow uniform and continuous cleaning. The spring-loaded shutter, which protects the media, is made of stainless steel.

The Manufacturing Process

The manufacture of a floppy disk takes place in three phases. First, the disk itself is made, then the case is made, and finally the two are assembled. The procedure for 8- and 5¼-inch disks differs slightly from that for the 3½-inch model.

Disk manufacture

1 First, the recording media (Mylar) is coated with an extremely fine layer of iron oxide. The thickness of this layer depends on the size of the disk and the type of density. For instance, the layer thickness is 110 microinches for 8-inch, high density diskettes and 35 microinches for 3½-inch high density disks. The coating for standard density diskettes is thicker than that for high density diskettes and is less coercive, meaning that it has less magnetic force.

2 Next, the coated Mylar film is cut and appropriate size disks are punched out by a machine that is similar to a cookie cutter. Each disk is then polished according to the required specifications and standards. Eight- and 5¼-inch disks can now be inserted into jackets. For

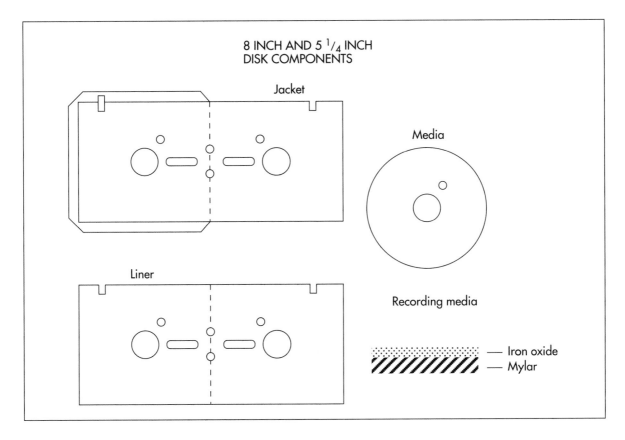

Jacket

Media

Liner

Recording media

— Iron oxide
— Mylar

Fig. 26. The major parts of 8-inch and 5¼-inch diskettes are the same. Both contain a recording media, a protective liner made of nonwoven fabric, and a soft plastic (PVC) jacket. The recording media consists of thin Mylar plastic with a coating layer of magnetic iron oxide.

3½-inch disks, a stainless steel hub is attached to the media with an adhesive ring. The disks are now ready for insertion into their plastic cases.

Jacket and case manufacture

3 The jackets of the 8-inch and 5¼-inch disks are cut out of polyvinyl chloride (PVC) to correct size, and the fabric liners laminated (glued) to them. Each jacket then has holes and notches punched in the appropriate places. The drive spindle hole in the middle helps to center the disk in the disk drive. The index hole, when lined up with another index hole punched in the media, permits the drive to locate the begin-

ning of each section of data. The long, thin, oval hole, also called the head access hole, is used by the magnetic head to come in direct contact with the media. The write protect notch prevents data from mistakenly being recorded or erased. The relief notches keep the lower end of the head access hole from bending. After the openings have been punched, the jacket is folded three ways, with only the top flap left open. The jackets are now ready for assembly.

4 The case or shell for $3\frac{1}{2}$-inch disk is molded out of hard plastic. It has a rectangular head access slot. The lower shell of the case is assembled with the button, the wiper tab, the write protect tab and the fabric liner. The upper fabric liner is attached to the upper shell. Now the spring-loaded shutter assembly is attached and the two shells are connected at the top two corners. The cases are now ready for assembly.

Disk and case assembly

5 For 8- and $5\frac{1}{4}$-inch disks, the media is inserted into the jacket through the top. Each disk then undergoes comprehensive electrical and mechanical testing and certification. After the top of the jacket, which had been left open, is folded, disk assembly is complete. Each disk is then given a final visual inspection before being labeled and packaged for shipment.

6 Assembly of $3\frac{1}{2}$-inch disks is very similar. First, the prepared media is inserted into the shell, and then the disk is tested and certified. The two shells are now welded (joined) at the bottom two corners and the assembly is complete. Each disk is given a final visual inspection and then labeled and packaged for shipment.

Quality Control

A floppy disk is a delicate device that must accurately record and play back the information stored on its recording media. Dust and scratches on the disk surface must be carefully avoided during the manufacturing process, as even the smallest imperfection can cause writing and reading errors. The manufacturing operation must be performed in a clean environment. As much of the process as possible is performed automatically, to minimize human contact with the disks.

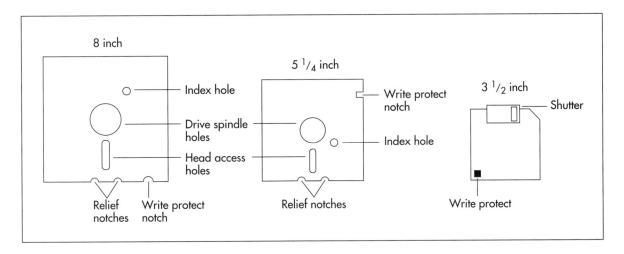

Fig. 27. This diagram shows fully assembled floppy disks in all 3 sizes. The relief notches on the 8- and 5 1/4-inch disks keep the head access hole from bending. The index hole allows the disk drive to locate the beginning of each section of data, while the drive spindle hole is used by the disk drive to center the recording media.

Quality control checkpoints are built into the process after each part is made or assembled. First, the coating mix is checked for proper viscosity (thickness, resistance to flow) and dispersion. Once the coating is applied, it is checked for thickness, surface tension, durability and coercivity (magnetic force). Punched-out disks are checked for proper size and placement of holes. The semi-assembled cases for 3 1/2-inch disks are checked for proper size, parts placement, shutter assembly function, and appearance. The semi-assembled jackets for the 8-inch and 5 1/4-inch disks are checked for proper sizes, hole and notch placement, and shape, seals, and appearance.

After the media has been inserted in the case, each disk is rigorously tested and goes through a certification process. Electrical testing checks the various electrical parameters (limits, boundaries) such as the recorded signal variance, recorded frequency, and format verification. Mechanical testing checks the various mechanical parameters such as weld strength, jacket durability, media durability, and dimensions (sizes and shapes).

The certification process ensures that there are no bad tracks on a disk (a track is the line the magnetic head follows in writing and reading data; the tracks form concentric circles). A disk that has been 100 percent certified has passed all tests on all tracks. Most manufacturers check every track of every disk and guarantee that each disk is error free.

Future Disks

In recent years, optoelectronic (using light and/or laser energy to read and write data) memories and storage devices have gained popularity for audio and video recordings, and the same technology is now being applied to computer memories. An optical disk is similar to a conventional disk except that the storage medium is thicker. Because of this difference, it is possible to record multiple images in one location on the disk.

Optical disks capable of storing up to 20 megabytes of data are already available, and research on higher-capacity disk technology is in progress. A recent experiment with a small $2\frac{1}{2}$-inch (6.35 centimeters) disk showed that as many as 1000 frames could be superimposed at one location on the disk. The storage capacity of the disk approaches about 10 pixels, which is the equivalent of about ten hours of regular video.

Such large storage capacity, combined with high speed data transfer and fast random access, makes optical memory a possible candidate for a wide range of applications such as image processing and database management. The future of floppy disk clearly lies in optical memories. Practical applications for this new technology may be available in the next three to five years.

WHERE TO LEARN MORE

Gralla, Preston. "Floppy Disks and Drives," *PC-Computing*. October 1992, pp. 324-25.

Macaulay, David. *The Way Things Work*. Houghton Mifflin Company, 1988.

Nimersheim, Jack. "Disk Anatomy," *Compute!* January 1990, pp. 58-62.

Guitar

How It Works

A member of the family of musical instruments called chordophones, the guitar is a stringed instrument which is played by "plucking" (pulling and releasing) a series of strings running along its body. As the strings are plucked with one hand, they are fingered with the other hand against frets, which are metal strips located on the instrument's neck. The resulting sound is amplified (increased) through a resonating (vibrating) body. There are four general categories of acoustic (non-electric) guitars: flat-top steel-stringed, arched top, classic, and flamenco.

Strings of the Past

Guitar-like instruments date back many centuries, and there is evidence that nearly every society throughout history has used some variation of the instrument. The forerunner of today's guitars were single-string bows developed during caveman times. In sections of Asia and Africa, bows of this type have been unearthed in archaeological digs of ancient civilizations. One of these discoveries includes a Hittite (an ancient society of people living in Syria and Asia Minor) carving—dating back more than 3,000 years—that shows an instrument with many of the same features of today's guitar: the curves of the body, a flat top with an arc of five sound holes on either side, and a long fretted neck that ran the entire length of the body.

As music technology developed, more strings were added to the early guitars. A four-string variety (named guitarra latina) existed in Spain in

Guitars are such an important part of the modern music scene that they've been called "the backbone of rock and roll."

Early hunters may have been responsible for inventing the guitar. Someone must have enjoyed the musical twang made by bow strings when arrows were shot at animals or enemies, because early instruments were like hunting bows.

the late thirteenth century. The guitarra latina closely resembled the ancient Hittite carving, but the instrument now included a thin, wooden bridge that held the strings in place as they passed over the soundhole. When a fifth string was added in the early sixteenth century, the guitar's popularity exploded. A sixth string (the bass E note) was added near the end of the 1700s, and brought the instrument closer to its present day appearance. The Carulli guitar of 1810 (named for an Italian composer of the time) was one of the first to have six single strings tuned to musical notes in the arrangement still used today: E A D G B E.

Guitar technology finally made its way to the United States in the early nineteenth century, when German guitar maker Charles Friedrich Martin immigrated to New York in 1833. In the early 1900s, the Martin Company—now located in Nazareth, Pennsylvania—produced large guitars that followed the design of classic models, especially the Spanish guitar. Another manufacturer, the Gibson company, began producing large steel-string guitars with arched (curved slightly outward) fronts and backs. Known as the cello guitar, this brand of instrument produced a sound well-suited to jazz and dance.

Guitar Materials

The back and sides of the guitar's body are usually built with East Indian or Brazilian rosewood (a dark or reddish hardwood with a strongly-marked grain that comes from a tropical tree). Historically, Brazilian rosewood has been the choice of experts. However, in an attempt to preserve their endangered supply, the Brazilian government has raised the price and placed restrictions on the export of rosewood. Currently East Indian rosewood is the best substitute. Less expensive guitar brands use wood from mahogany or maple trees, but the sound quality suffers in guitars constructed with those types of wood.

The top (or soundboard) of the guitar is traditionally constructed of Alpine spruce (an evergreen tree), although American Sika spruce has become popular among U.S. manufacturers. Cedar and redwood are often substituted for spruce, but these woods are soft and easily damaged during construction.

The neck, which must resist bending or distortion by the pull of the strings and changes in temperature and humidity, is made from mahogany and joins the body between the fourteenth and twelfth frets. Ideally, the fingerboard is made of ebony, but rosewood is often used as a less expensive substitute. Most modern guitars use strings made of some type of metal (usually steel).

The Manufacturing Process

The first and most important step in guitar construction is wood selection. The choice of wood will directly affect the sound quality of the finished instrument. The wood must be free of flaws and have a straight, vertical (up and down) grain. Since each section of the guitar uses different types of woods, the construction process varies from section to section. Following is a description of the manufacture of a typical acoustic guitar.

A modern acoustic guitar.

Bookmatching

1 The wood for the top of the guitar is cut from lumber using a process called bookmatching. Bookmatching is a method by which a single piece of wood is sliced into two sheets, each the same length and width as the original but only half as thick. This produces two sheets of wood with a symmetrical (matching) grain pattern. The two sheets are laid flat, side-by-side (like the open pages of a book), lined up to ensure that the grain patterns match and meet exactly, then glued together. Once dry, the newly joined boards are sanded to the proper thickness. They are closely inspected for quality and then graded according to color, closeness and regularity of grain, and lack of flaws.

2 The next step is to cut the top into the guitar shape, leaving the piece of wood oversized until the final trimming. The soundhole is sawed, with slots carved around it for concentric circles (each enclosing the last in a bull's eye pattern). These will hold or serve as decorations around the soundhole.

Strutting

3 Wood braces are then glued to the underside of the top piece. Strutting, as this process is often called, serves two purposes: to brace the wood against the pull of the strings, and to control the way the top vibrates. An area of guitar construction that differs from company to company, strutting has a great effect on the guitar's tone. Many braces today are glued in an X-pattern originally designed by the Martin Company, a pattern that most experts feel provides the truest acoustics (sounds) and tone. Although other companies continue to experiment with improvements on the X-pattern style of strutting, Martin's concept is widely known for producing the best sound.

4 The back, although not as acoustically important as the top, is still very important to the guitar's sound. A reflector of sound waves, the back is also braced, but its strips of wood run parallel from left to right with one cross-grained strip running down the length of the back's center glue joint. The back is cut and glued, much like the top (using the bookmatch technique)—and from the same piece of lumber as the top, to ensure matching grains.

Constructing the sides

5 Construction of the sides consists of cutting and sanding the strips of wood to the proper length and thickness, then softening the wood in water. The strips are then placed in molds that match the curves of the guitar, and the entire assembly is clamped in place for a period of time to ensure symmetry (matching curves) between the two sides. The two sides are joined together with basswood (a North American tree with soft, light-colored wood) glued to the inside walls. Strips of wood are placed along the inner sides so that the guitar doesn't crack if hit from the side. Two endblocks (near the neck and near the bottom of the guitar) are also used to join the top, back, and neck.

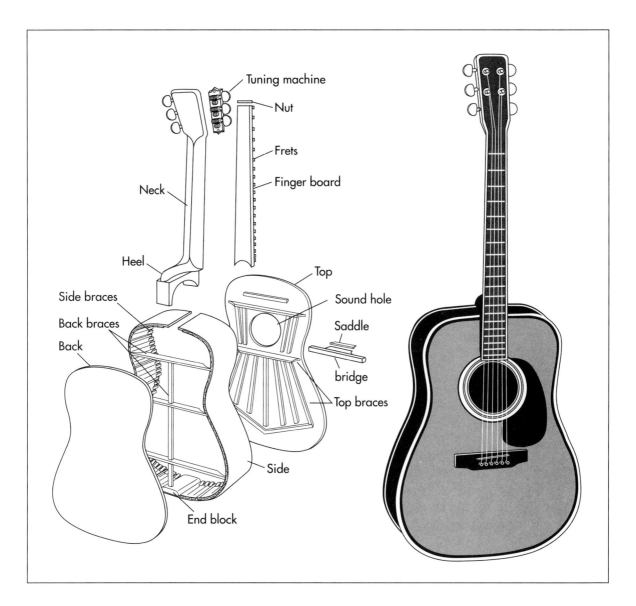

Fig. 28. Guitar manufacture generally involves selecting, sawing, and gluing various wood pieces to form the finished instrument.

6 Once the sides are joined and the endblocks are in place, the top and the back are glued to the sides. The excess wood is trimmed off and slots are cut along the lines where the side/top and side/back meet. These slots are for the body bindings that cover the guitar's sides. The

bindings are not only decorative, but they also keep moisture from entering through the sides and warping the guitar.

Neck and fingerboard

7 The guitar's neck is made from one piece of hard wood, typically mahogany or rosewood, carved to exact specifications. A rod is inserted through the length of the neck to make it stronger and, after sanding, the fingerboard (often made of ebony or rosewood) is set in place. Using precise measurements, fret slots are cut into the fingerboard and the steel-wired frets are put in place.

8 Once the neck construction is complete, it is attached to the body. Most guitar companies attach the neck and the body by fitting a "heel" that extends from the base of the neck into a pre-cut groove on the body. Once the glue has dried at the neck-body connection, the entire guitar receives a coat of clear sealer and several coats of lacquer (a transparent coating which dries to a hard gloss) to protect the wood. On some models, colorful decorations are glued on or set into the guitar top.

Bridge and saddle

9 After polishing, a bridge is attached near the bottom of the guitar below the soundhole, and a saddle is fitted. The saddle is where the strings actually lie as they pass over the bridge, and it is extremely important in the transferring of string vibration to the guitar top. On the opposite end of the guitar, the nut is placed between the neck and the head. The nut is a strip of wood or plastic on which the strings lie as they pass to the head and into the tuning machine.

Bob Dylan playing guitar as part of President Bill Clinton's inaugural festivities, 1993.

Tuning machine

10 Next, the tuning machine is fitted to the guitar head. This machine is one of the most delicate parts of the guitar and is usually mounted on the back of the head. The pegs that hold each string poke through to the front, and the gears that turn both the pegs and the string-tightening keys are enclosed in metal casings.

11 Finally, the guitar is strung and inspected before leaving the factory. The entire process of making a guitar can take between three weeks and two months, depending on the amount of decorative detail work on the guitar top.

A Les Paul Custom guitar.

Electric Guitars

A different but closely related group of guitars is the electric guitar, which uses a device known as a pickup—a magnet surrounded by wire—to convert the energy from string vibrations into an electrical signal. The signal is sent to an amplifier, where it is boosted thousands of times. The body of an electric guitar has little influence on the quality of sound produced, since the amplifier controls both the quality and loudness of the sound.

Acoustic guitars can also be fitted with electric pickups, and there are some models available today that have the pickup built into the body. Guitarists who prefer acoustic instruments, but need the louder sound for a concert stage, often choose this acoustical electric guitar.

Quality Control

Most guitar manufacturers are small companies that stress detail and quality. Each company does its own research and testing, which ensures

Some master luthiers inset distinctive, decorative mosaics on their guitar tops. They contain hundreds, sometimes thousands of very tiny, stained pieces of wood, shell, or pearl arranged into a particular, unique pattern—usually a flower or circular design.

the customer of a flawless guitar. During the past few decades, the guitar industry has become more mechanized, allowing for greater speed, higher consistency, and lower pricing. Although purists (those who prefer traditional methods and products) resist mechanization, a well-trained workman using machine tools can often produce a higher-quality instrument than a craftsman working alone.

The final testing procedures at most manufacturers are quite strict. Only the best guitars leave the plant, and more than one person makes the final decision as to which instruments are shipped out and which are rejected.

WHERE TO LEARN MORE

Ardley, Neil. *Eyewitness Books: Music.* Alfred A. Knopf, 1989.

Evans, Tom and Mary Anne. *Guitars: Music, History, Construction and Players from the Renaissance to Rock.* Facts on File, 1977.

How It Works: The Illustrated Science and Invention Encyclopedia. Vol. 9. H.S. Stuttman, 1983.

Klenck, Thomas. "Shop Project: Electric Guitar," *Popular Mechanics.* September 1990, pp. 43-48.

Macauley, David. *The Way Things Work.* Houghton Mifflin Company, 1988.

Helicopter

Vertical Flight

Helicopters are considered to be rotary wing aircraft because their "wings" (rotor blades) spin on an axis or motorized shaft. The rotating wing is commonly called the main rotor or simply the rotor. Unlike the more common fixed wing aircraft, the helicopter is capable of vertical (up and down) take-off and landing. It can also hover (stop in mid-air) in a fixed position. These features make helicopters ideal for use where space is limited or where the ability to hover over a certain area is necessary.

Currently, helicopters are used for a wide variety of jobs. They are the best vehicle for dusting crops with pesticides or fertilizers, reaching remote areas for environmental work, and delivering supplies to workers on oil rigs which are located far out at sea. They are useful for taking photographs, filming movies, and rescuing people trapped in almost unreachable spots (for example, in mountains, or on water). They have saved lives through fast transport of accident victims to hospitals and by helping to douse raging fires. They are also used by government for intelligence (spying) and military (wartime defense) applications.

The idea for the helicopter appears to have been an attempt to imitate the vertical flight of the whirling, two-winged seed (fruit) of the maple tree.

Origin

Many scientists and inventors have contributed to the concepts and development of the helicopter. The idea appears to have a bionic origin, meaning that it came from an attempt to adapt a natural principal—in this case, the whirling, two-winged fruit (or seed) of the maple tree—to a mechanical design. Early efforts to imitate maple pods produced the

A Bell Jet Ranger helicopter.

whirligig, a children's toy popular in China as well as in medieval Europe.

During the fifteenth century, Leonardo da Vinci, the famous Italian painter, sculptor, architect, and engineer, sketched a flying machine that may have been based on the whirligig. The next surviving sketch of a helicopter dates from the early nineteenth century, when British scientist Sir George Cayley drew a twin-rotor aircraft in his notebook.

Early Flying Attempts

Frenchman Paul Cornu, during the early twentieth century, managed to lift himself off the ground for a few seconds in an early helicopter. However, Cornu was grounded by the same problems that would continue to aggravate all early designers for several decades. No one had yet invented an engine that could cause a strong enough vertical thrust to lift both the helicopter and any significant load (including passengers) off the ground.

A U.S. Navy helicopter flies over the USS *Independence*.

Igor Sikorsky, a Russian engineer, built his first helicopter in 1909. When neither this first machine nor his second in 1910 were successful, Sikorsky decided that he could not build a helicopter without more sophisticated materials and money, so he turned his attention to building airplanes.

During World War I, Hungarian engineer Theodore von Karman constructed a helicopter that, when tethered (attached to a cable or chain), was able to hover for extended periods.

Several years later, Spaniard Juan de la Cierva developed a machine he called an autogiro to correct the tendency of conventional airplanes to lose engine power and crash when landing. If he could design an aircraft in which lift and thrust (forward speed) were separate functions, Cierva thought he could overcome this problem. The autogiro he eventually invented included features of both the helicopter and the airplane.

The autogiro had a rotor that functioned something like a windmill. Once set in motion by starting off slowly on the ground, the rotor could create extra lift. However, the autogiro was powered primarily by a conventional airplane engine. To avoid landing problems, the engine was turned off and the autogiro lowered gently to the ground by the rotor blade, which gradually stopped spinning as the machine reached the ground. Popular during the 1920s and 1930s, autogiros disappeared from use after the development of the helicopter.

The helicopter was eventually perfected by Igor Sikorsky. Advances in aerodynamics (interaction of air or atmosphere with moving objects) and building materials had been made since Sikorsky's first efforts, and, in 1939, he lifted off the ground in his first successful helicopter. Two years later, an improved design enabled him to remain above ground for an hour and a half, setting a world record for nonstop helicopter flight.

The helicopter was put to military use almost immediately after its introduction. The challenges of warfare in the jungle regions of both Korea and Vietnam prompted the helicopter's widespread use during both of those wars. Technological improvements made it a valuable tool during the Persian Gulf War as well.

In recent years, however, private industry has probably been responsible for the greatest increase in helicopter use. Many companies have begun to transport their managers by helicopter. In addition, helicopter shuttle services are operating successfully along routes between major cities. Still, among everyday travelers the helicopter remains best known for medical, rescue, and relief work.

Whirlybird Works

A helicopter's power comes from an engine which moves the rotor shaft, causing the blades to turn. While a standard plane produces thrust by pushing air behind its wing as it moves forward, the helicopter's rotor achieves lift by pushing the air beneath it downward as it spins. Lift is related to change in the air's momentum (its mass or amount times its speed): the greater the momentum, the greater the lift.

Helicopter rotor systems consist of between two and six blades attached to a central hub. Usually long and narrow, the blades turn rather slowly, because this minimizes the amount of power necessary to achieve and maintain lift. The low speed also makes controlling the vehicle easier. While lightweight, general-purpose helicopters often have a two-bladed main rotor; heavier craft may use a four-blade design or two separate main rotors to handle heavy loads.

A helicopter floating in New York's East River after making an emergency landing, 1991.

To steer a helicopter, the pilot must adjust the pitch (angle) of the blades, which can be set three ways. In the collective system, the pitch of all the blades attached to the rotor is identical; in the cyclic system, the pitch of each blade is designed to change as the rotor revolves, and the third system uses a combination of the first two. To move the helicopter in any direction, the pilot moves the lever that adjusts collective pitch and/or the stick that adjusts cyclic pitch; it may also be necessary to increase or reduce speed.

Unlike airplanes, which are designed to eliminate extra bulk and projections that would weigh the craft down and interrupt airflow around it, helicopters have unavoidably high "drag." This means they have lots of parts which stick out at odd angles, "dragging" against the air as they move, slowing them down. Helicopter designers have not used the sort of retractable landing gear familiar to people who have watched planes taking off or landing—these gears can be pulled into the plane as it takes off, and thrust out before landing causing the body to be more streamlined.

NOTAR helicopters have extra advantages. Without the whirling tail rotor blades, they are much quieter and safer than other designs.

The aerodynamic gains of such a system would not be as significant for a helicopter.

In general, helicopter landing gear is much simpler than that of airplanes. Airplanes need long runways on which to reduce forward speed. Helicopters have to reduce only vertical lift, which they can do by hovering before landing. Thus, they don't even require shock absorbers: their landing gear usually consists only of wheels or skids (a type of brake or runner), or both.

One problem associated with helicopter rotor blades occurs because airflow along the length of each blade differs widely. This means that lift and drag change for each blade throughout its rotation, causing an unsteady ride for the helicopter. A related problem occurs when, as the helicopter moves forward, the lift beneath the blades that enter the airstream first is high, but beneath the blades on the opposite side of the rotor it is low. These problems cause instability in the helicopter. Manufacturers make up for these unpredictable variations in lift and drag by designing flexible blades connected to the rotor by a hinge. This design allows each blade to shift up or down, adjusting to changes in lift and drag.

Torque (the turning, twisting force) is another problem associated with a rotating wing. Torque causes the helicopter fuselage (cabin) to rotate in the opposite direction from the rotor, especially when the helicopter is moving at low speeds or hovering. To offset this reaction, many helicopters use a tail rotor, an exposed blade or fan mounted on the end of its long tail. Another means of correcting torque involves installing two rotors, attached to the same engine but rotating in opposite directions. A third, more space-efficient design features twin rotors that fit together—something like an egg beater. Additional alternatives have been researched, and at least one NOTAR (no tail rotor) design has been introduced.

Helicopter Materials

The airframe, or basic structure, of a helicopter can be made of either metal or organic composite materials, or some combination of the two.

When designing a helicopter that will carry heavy loads, manufacturers choose materials that are especially strong but relatively lightweight. Some of these materials are epoxy (a resin—thick, sticky, transparent substance found in plants and used in making plastics) reinforced with glass, aramid (a strong, flexible nylon fiber), or carbon (a natural non-metallic element) fiber. Typically, these materials consist of many layers of resins with fibers added for strength, that are joined or glued together to form a smooth panel.

Tubular (hollow cylinder) and sheet metal sections of the helicopter are usually made of aluminum, though stainless steel or titanium (a strong, light-weight metal) are sometimes used in areas that must accept higher stress or heat. To ease bending during the manufacturing process, the metal tubing is often filled with molten sodium silicate (also called water glass—a glass-like mixture heated to a melted state). A helicopter's rotary wing blades are usually made of fiber-reinforced resin, which may have a sheet metal layer glued to the outside to protect the edges. The helicopter's windscreen and windows are formed of polycarbonate sheeting (high-impact plastic).

The Manufacturing Process

Airframe: Preparing the tubing

1 Each individual tubular part is cut by a tube-cutting machine that can be quickly set to produce different, precise lengths and quantities. Tubing that must be bent is shaped to the proper angle in a bending machine that uses interchangeable tools for different diameters and sizes.

For major bends, tubes are filled with molten sodium silicate that hardens and eliminates kinking by causing the tube to bend as a solid bar. This so-called water glass is then removed by placing the bent tube in boiling water, which melts the inner material and allows it to drain out. Tubing that must be curved to match cabin shapes is fitted over a stretch forming machine, which stretches the metal to a precise shape.

Next, the tubular details are delivered to the machine shop where they are held in clamps so that their ends can be finished to the required angle and shape. The tubes are then deburred (a process in which any ridges or points that remain are ground off), then inspected for cracks.

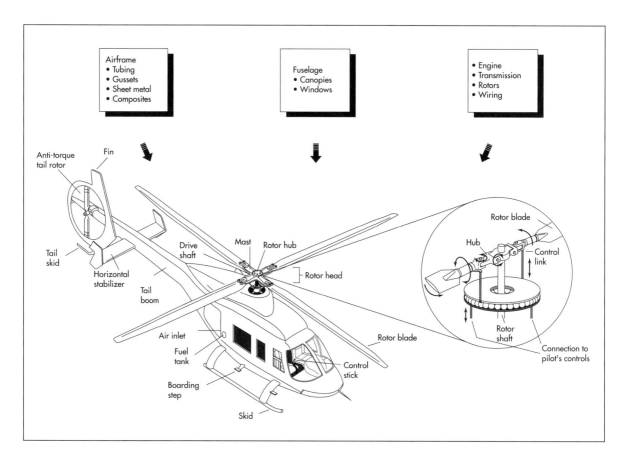

Airframe
• Tubing
• Gussets
• Sheet metal
• Composites

Fuselage
• Canopies
• Windows

• Engine
• Transmission
• Rotors
• Wiring

Anti-torque tail rotor

Fin

Tail skid

Horizontal stabilizer

Tail boom

Drive shaft

Mast

Rotor hub

Rotor head

Air inlet

Fuel tank

Boarding step

Control stick

Skid

Rotor blade

Rotor blade

Hub

Control link

Rotor shaft

Connection to pilot's controls

Fig. 29. Most of the crucial components in a helicopter are made of metal and are formed using the usual metal-forming processes: shearing, blanking, forging, cutting, routing, and casting. The polycarbonate windscreen and windows are made by laying the sheet over a mold, heating it, and forming it with air pressure in a process called "freeblowing," in which no tool ever touches the part.

2 Reinforcing metal parts are made by machines which rout (hollow out), shear (cut), blank (punch or stamp), or saw. Some complex details may be forged (heated and formed) or cast.

After they are removed and cooled, these parts are finished and deburred once again.

3 The tubes are cleaned with strong chemicals and welded into place. After welding, the assembled part is stress relieved—heated to a low temperature so that the metal can recover any elasticity it has lost during the shaping process. Finally, the welds are inspected for flaws.

Forming sheet metal details

4 Sheet metal, which makes up other parts of the airframe, is first cut into blanks (pieces cut to appropriate size in preparation for more work). Aluminum blanks are heat-treated to anneal them (make the metal tough but bendable). The blanks are then refrigerated until they are placed in dies where they will be pressed into the proper shape. After forming, the sheet metal details are aged to full strength and trimmed to final shape and size.

Casting involves injecting wax or an alloy (metal mixture) with a low melting point into a mold or die. When the pattern has been formed, it is dipped in molten metal as many times as necessary to achieve the thickness desired. When the part has dried, it is heated so that the wax or alloy will melt and can be poured out. The mold is heated to a higher temperature to purify it and placed in a mold box where it is supported by sand. Then the mold is ready to shape molten metal into reinforcement parts.

5 Sheet metal parts are cleaned before being bolted or glued. Aluminum parts and welded subassemblies may be anodized (treated to thicken the protective oxide film on the surface of the aluminum), which increases corrosion resistance. All metal parts are chemically cleaned and primer-painted, and most are finished by spraying with an epoxy or other durable coating.

Making the cores of composite components

6 Cores, the central parts of the composite components (sections of the helicopter constructed of many parts) are made of Nomex (a brand of aramid—nylon fiber— produced by Du Pont) or aluminum "honeycomb," which is cut to size by a band saw or knife. If necessary, the cores have their edges trimmed and cut to an angle by a machine tool similar to a pizza cutter or meat slicing blade.

The material with which each component is built up from its core is called pre-preg ply. The plies are layers of fibers that have been strengthened with resin. Following written instructions from the designers, workers create carefully shaped "skin" panels by setting individual plies on bond mold tools and sandwiching cores between additional plies as directed.

7 Completed layups, as the layers of pre-preg glued to the mold are called, are then transported to an autoclave for curing. An autoclave is a machine that joins layers of plastics by exposing them to pressurized steam, and "curing" is the hardening that occurs as the resin layers "cook" in the autoclave.

8 Visible trim lines are molded into the panels. Extra material around the edges is removed by power sawing. Large panels may be trimmed by an abrasive waterjet, handled by a robot. After inspection, trimmed panels and other composite details are cleaned and painted by normal spray methods. Surfaces must be well sealed by paint to prevent metal corrosion or water absorption.

Making the fuselage

9 Tops or windscreens and passenger compartment windows are generally made of polycarbonate sheeting. Front panels subject to bird strike or other impact may be laminated of two sheets for greater thickness. All such parts are made by placing an oversized blank on a fixture, heating it, and then forming it to the required curvature by use of air pressure in a freeblowing process. In this method, to avoid defects, no tool touches the surface.

Installing the engine, transmission, and rotors

10 Modern helicopter engines are purchased from an engine supplier. The helicopter manufacturer may buy or produce the transmission assembly, which transfers power to the rotor assembly. Transmission cases are made of aluminum or magnesium mixtures (alloy).

11 As with the above, the main and tail rotor assemblies are made by machine from specially selected high-strength metals. Main rotor blades may have a sheet metal layer glued on to protect the leading edges.

Systems and controls

12 Electric wires that connect systems for helicopters must be enclosed in protective coverings called wiring harnesses. They are produced by laying out the required wires on special boards that serve as patterns to define the length and path to connectors. Looms, or knitted protective covers, are placed on the wire bundles, and the purchased connectors are soldered (cemented with melted tin or lead) in place by hand. Tubing is either hand-cut to length and hand-formed by craftsmen, or measured, formed, and cut by tube-bending machines. Ends are flared, and tubes are inspected for accuracy of size and to ensure that no cracks are present. Hydraulic (using fluids) pumps and actuators, instrumentation, and electrical devices are typically made to order by companies that specialize in their production, then purchased by the helicopter manufacturer for installation.

Final assembly

13 Finished and inspected airframe parts, including sheet metal, tubular, machined, and welded items, are delivered to subassembly jigs (fixtures that clamp parts being assembled in place). Central parts are located in each jig, and connecting parts are either bolted in place or riveted with power drills. For aerodynamic smoothness on sheet metal or skin panels, holes are sunken so that the tops of flat-headed screws won't stick up. All holes are deburred and rivets applied. A sealant is often applied in each hole as the rivet is inserted. Some manufacturers use semi-automated machines for each process; a worker moves from one hole location to the next, drilling, sealing, and installing the rivets.

14 After each subassembly is accepted by an inspector, it typically moves to another jig to be further combined with other small subassemblies and details such as brackets. Inspected "top level" subassemblies are then delivered to final assembly jigs, where the overall helicopter structure is built.

Upon completion of the structure, the engine parts are added, then wiring and hydraulics are installed and tested. Canopy, windows, doors, instruments, and interior elements are then added to complete the vehicle. Finish-painting and trimming are completed at appropriate points during this process.

15 After all systems are inspected in final form, the complete documentation (records) of materials, processes, inspection, and rework effort for each vehicle is checked and filed for future reference. The helicopter propulsion system (engine and parts that drive or propel it) is checked, and the aircraft is flight-tested.

Quality Control

Once tubular components have been formed, they are inspected for cracks. To find defects, workers treat the tubes with a fluorescent liquid that seeps into cracks and other surface flaws. After wiping off the excess fluid, they dust the coated tube with a fine powder that interacts with the liquid to make defects stand out.

After the tubular components have been welded, they are inspected using X-ray and/or fluorescent inspection methods to find flaws. Upon completion, the curves of sheet metal details are checked against form patterns and hand-worked to fit. After they have been autoclaved (see step 7) and trimmed, composite panels are inspected to identify any possible breaks in laminations or other flaws that could lead to structural failure.

Before installation, both the engine and the transmission subassemblies are carefully inspected. Special testing equipment, custom-designed for each application, is used to examine the wiring systems. All of the other components are also tested before assembly, and the completed aircraft is flight-tested in addition to receiving an overall inspection.

Helicopters of the Future

Manufacturing processes and techniques will continue to change in response to the need to reduce costs and the introduction of new materials. Automation may further improve quality and lower labor costs. Computers will become more important in improving designs, making design changes, and reducing the amount of paperwork created, used, and stored for each helicopter built.

Furthermore, the use of robots to wind filament (fine wire or fiber), wrap tape, and place fiber will permit cabin structures to be made of fewer pieces. Advanced, high-strength thermoplastic resins promise greater impact resistance and repairability than current materials used. New metallic composites also promise higher strength-to-weight ratios for critical parts such as transmission cases while keeping the heat resistance advantage of metal over organic (natural) materials.

WHERE TO LEARN MORE

Cooper, Chris, and Jane Insley. *How Does It Work?* Orbis Publishing, 1986.
Kerrod, Robin. *Visual Science: METALS.* Silver Burdett Company, 1982.
Library of Science Technology. Marshall Cavendish Corporation, 1989.

Macaulay, David. *The Way Things Work*. Houghton Mifflin Company, 1988.

Patrick, Michael. "Roto Scooter," *Popular Mechanics*. February 1993, pp. 32-35.

Reader's Digest: How in the World? Reader's Digest, 1990.

Index

Boldfacing
indicates entrants

Bynema 49